Arryn,

Be grateful and remember
you are loved and blessed.

I Love You
Always and Forever

* Be sure to read a
daily devotion *

From:

Mom

Message:

I am grateful for
You! One of my most precious many
Gifts and Blessings

Mini Devotions for Women
Published by Christian Art Publishers
PO Box 1599, Vereeniging, 1930, RSA

© 2019
First edition 2019

Devotions taken from *One-Minute Devotions® for Women*

Designed by Christian Art Publishers

Cover designed by Christian Art Publishers

Images used under license from Shutterstock.com

Scripture taken from Scripture quotations taken from the *Holy Bible*,
New International Version®, NIV® Copyright © 1973, 1978, 1984,
2011 by Biblica, Inc.® Used by permission. All rights reserved worldwide

Printed in China

ISBN 978-1-4321-3139-5

21 22 23 24 25 26 27 28 29 30 – 14 13 12 11 10 9 8 7 6 5

MINI DEVOTIONS
for Women

CAROLYN LARSEN

CHRISTIAN ART
PUBLISHERS

Outside the Church

> They asked his disciples, "Why does your
> teacher eat with tax collectors and sinners?"
> On hearing this, Jesus said, "It is not the
> healthy who need a doctor, but the sick."
>
> *Matthew 9:11-12*

The church isn't just here for Christians. Jesus' statement reminds us that we shouldn't get comfortably settled in our pews and let the world go by.

Jesus went out to where the people were who needed to know that God loved them. He spent time with the "undesirables" of His day. We must be careful not to get comfortable in our church where we all look the same, believe the same, and have the same social standards.

We must remember that there is a whole world full of people who don't yet know about God's love. It's up to us to tell them.

A Living Faith

In the same way, faith by itself, if it
is not accompanied by action, is dead.

James 2:17

Actions speak louder than words. Talking about your
faith to other people is one thing. But a real, living
faith demands action. Just the word "living" implies
activity of some kind.

Coming face to face with the love of God, profes-
sing faith in Him, and understanding the permanence
and consequences of eternity in hell should bring us
to action. That action should be an eagerness to tell
everyone we come into contact with about God's
love and forgiveness.

The fact that our faith brings action confirms
that it is real, living faith. Faith is good; faith without
action is not good.

No Silence!

You are a chosen people, a royal priesthood,
a holy nation, a people belonging to God,
that you may declare the praises of him who
called you out of darkness into his wonderful light.

1 Peter 2:9

Doesn't this verse make you feel special? God – the Creator of the entire Universe – chose you. He chose you! You belong to Him. What could be more special than that? But He didn't choose you to sit quietly in a room with stained-glass windows. He chose you so that you can declare His praises.

He wants you to tell people how He called you out of darkness and into light. That's called witnessing. God doesn't want you to be silent about what He has done for you.

Patient Fisherman

"Come, follow me," Jesus said,
"and I will make you fishers of men."

Matthew 4:19

Fishing takes patience. You can sit in the boat or on the dock for hours at a time before you actually catch a fish; in fact sometimes you don't catch one at all. But usually patience and diligence pay off. So, it's interesting that Jesus used fishing to describe the process of winning people to Him. He promises to make us fishermen.

God has given each of us unique gifts and talents and Jesus uses those to make each of us fishermen. We work within our strengths. He doesn't ask us to do things He has not given us the ability to do.

It takes patience and diligence, but the reward is seeing souls come to Him!

Team Colors

Never be lacking in zeal, but keep
your spiritual fervor, serving the Lord.

Romans 12:11

Turn on the television any Sunday afternoon in November or December and you will observe thousands of people with zeal! They cheer for their favorite football team, dress in the team colors, wear silly hats, and perhaps even paint their faces in the team colors. They are passionate about their team.

Can you imagine Christians with crosses painted on their faces, wearing team shirts, shouting out praises to Jesus? Can you see them going into the neighborhood and spreading their enthusiasm for the Lord?

Paul encouraged us to keep our zeal and our fervor – our joy in serving the Lord. It's the excitement and joy that will draw others to want to know Christ.

A Position of Honor

We are therefore Christ's ambassadors,
as though God were making his appeal
through us. We implore you on Christ's
behalf: Be reconciled to God.

2 Corinthians 5:20

An ambassador represents his home country in a foreign land. He speaks for his government and attends official functions on the president's behalf. It is a position of authority and honor.

We are Christ's ambassadors; His representatives in this world. He desires to speak through us, sharing the gospel message of hope and salvation with the world. We must make ourselves available to Him. The almighty God can certainly accomplish His purposes without us. But we have been given a position of honor and responsibility to be available for God to use us to encourage people to be reconciled to Him.

Be Ready

Do your best to present yourself to
God as one approved, a workman
who does not need to be ashamed and
who correctly handles the word of truth.

2 Timothy 2:15

Do not take your position as God's workman lightly. It comes with a responsibility. If God has given you the privilege of sharing the truths of His Word with others, be sure you are doing it correctly.

As you mark out a path for others to walk down on their journey to knowing Jesus, be careful to study God's Word and correctly present it.

This verse isn't meant to scare you away from witnessing, only to take the privilege of sharing God's message seriously and to always be prepared.

A Good Defense

In your hearts set apart Christ as Lord.
Always be prepared to give an answer
to everyone who asks you to give
the reason for the hope that you have.

1 Peter 3:15

The best defense is a good offense. We live in a sophisticated world where education and intelligence are highly valued. In order to share the message of salvation with people, you must be ready to share and you must know what you're talking about.

Take advantage of learning opportunities in your church in order to have a clearer understanding of the Bible and be able to articulately defend your faith. Hopefully, you will also have practical life examples of how God interacts in the world.

Knowledge and experience are two key ingredients for giving the reason for the hope that you have.

Come Forward, Workers

"The harvest is plentiful but the workers
are few. Ask the Lord of the harvest, therefore
to send out workers into his harvest field."

Matthew 9:37-38

God, in His infinite wisdom, decided to allow us, His children, to participate in the process of bringing other people to Him. It's a privilege we take all too lightly these days.

Jesus knew that there were plenty of people who needed to hear the gospel message and, in fact, were waiting to hear it. But the workers were not coming forward. He asked His disciples to pray for workers to come forward.

We must do the same ... pray for workers who are willing to leave their homes, and possibly their homelands, to share the message of God's love with all who will listen.

Growing Believers

I planted the seed, Apollos
watered it, but God made it grow.

1 Corinthians 3:6

God gives each of us gifts and talents. Some of us are seed planters, making an initial contact with a person, perhaps giving them their first contact with a Christian.

Another person is the one who waters. This person has a longer contact with the unbeliever, gently watering the seed that was planted, waiting for the water to settle, then watering again.

Each of us must do our job and we must work as a team for a seed to be planted. However, it is not any of our responsibility to make the seed grow – only God can do that. If we each do our jobs, He will do the rest.

Be Ready

Preach the Word; be prepared in season
and out of season; correct, rebuke and encourage –
with great patience and careful instruction.

2 Timothy 4:2

Do you read this verse and think, "But, I'm no minister!"
You don't have to be. But, as a believer, you do need
to read God's Word and learn how it applies to your
life. What you learn are lessons that can be shared in
everyday conversation and friendship.

Know the Word, be ready to share it – when it's
easy and when it isn't. Gently use God's Word to show
the right way to live and the right choices to make.

Be careful to be patient with those you share
with. Be careful to correctly give instructions from
the Word. Be careful, but be firm.

Don't Be Lazy

A curse on him who is lax
in doing the LORD's work!

Jeremiah 48:10

Whoa! This is serious. God does not kid around about His work. He doesn't save us so that we can sit down in a padded pew, hold a hymnal in front of our faces and take a nap. There is work to do and God wants us to do it.

God does not want anyone in the entire world to die without having had the opportunity to hear about Him and His love.

How will people hear if we don't tell them? Don't be lazy. Don't be afraid. Just get up and get busy doing the job God has given you for this day.

Do the Lord's work.

Get Busy!

"As long as it is day, we must do the
work of him who sent me. Night
is coming, when no one can work."

John 9:4

Jesus spoke these words to encourage His followers
to get busy. There is work to be done and that work
is to win others to God.

Jesus Himself was busy with that work the whole
time He walked this earth. He warns that a time is
coming when it will be too late to share the gospel.
No one will be able to respond to it in that day.

Do you sense the urgency? Get up, get busy and do
the work God gave you to do while there is still time.
When night comes ... when the time for deciding is
over ... it's too late.

Practical Advice

Carry each other's burdens, and in this
way you will fulfill the law of Christ.

Galatians 6:2

Christ taught that the greatest commandment is to love God with all your heart, soul, and mind and the second is to love your neighbor as yourself. When another person is hurting and you have the ability or wherewithal to help that person ... do it. That may be the most effective witness you can give.

You can stand in front of a hurting person and preach about God's love ... but putting your message into action and actually helping her will probably go a lot farther than just your words would.

Share Christ's love in real ways, then add the words to your action for a complete message.

A "How-To"

Your word is a lamp to my
feet and a light for my path.

Psalm 119:105

"I want to witness for God, but I just don't know what to do or say!" Here's the antidote for those feelings: Let God guide your steps and your words. Ask Him to direct you to someone who needs to know about Him. Ask Him to give you the correct words to say.

Spend time in His Word so you know it and can share from it the truth that every person is a sinner, Christ died for our sins and rose again.

Know His Word so you can share the plan of salvation from it. Be able to share examples of how God has guided your footsteps through His Word.

Party On!

"If he finds it, I tell you the truth, he is happier
about that one sheep than about the ninety-nine
that did not wander off. In the same way
your Father in heaven is not willing that
any of these little ones should be lost."

Matthew 18:13-14

Jesus had just shared the parable of the lost sheep with
His disciples. This parable recounts how a shepherd
had 100 sheep and one got lost. He left the ninety-nine
to go and find that one lost sheep. When he found
it, he celebrated with joy.

Jesus said that God feels that way about people.
He doesn't want anyone to be lost for eternity – not
even one person. That means that He wants all people
to have the opportunity to choose to accept the
gospel message.

If the whole world is going to hear the gospel, we'd
better get busy!

The Best Gift

Praise be to the LORD, for he
showed his wonderful love to me.

Psalm 31:21

What is the most wonderful gift you have ever been given? Think about it for a minute. What made it so special? Who gave it to you? After you received it, what did you do? Did you tell anyone? Did you celebrate?

The most wonderful gift imaginable is the truth that God loves you. He loves you unconditionally, completely, and eternally. What kind of response does that evoke in your heart? Are you going to keep quiet about His love? Do you feel like celebrating? How about sharing? It's certainly not something you can keep quiet about, right?

Then tell someone today about His wonderful love. Tell how you are aware of His love in your daily life.

Witness!

You will receive power when the Holy
Spirit comes on you; and you will be
my witnesses in Jerusalem, and in all Judea
and Samaria, and to the ends of the earth.

Acts 1:8

A couple of important observations from this verse: One, Jesus doesn't say, "You might be my witnesses ... or some of you will be my witnesses." He says you will be my witnesses.

The second thing is that we don't have to be a witness in our own strength. He sent the Holy Spirit to help us do this work. The bottom line is that we're all witnesses for something – whatever is most important to us in life.

Are you witnessing for Jesus or for something like well-decorated houses? Make sure your witness is for Jesus, then ask Him where He wants you to do the witnessing.

Great Commission

"Therefore, go and make disciples of all
nations, baptizing them in the name
of the Father and of the Son and of the Holy
Spirit and teaching them to obey everything
I have commanded you. And surely, I am
with you always, to the very end of the age."

Matthew 28:19-20

Through the years this passage has come to be known as The Great Commission and it is often used at mission conferences to try to motivate people to take up missionary service. It certainly leaves no doubt as to what is important to Jesus.

The command is plain – He wants all nations to know Him and follow Him. He wants all nations to be taught to obey God. These verses leave no doubt as to how we should be spending our time.

The assurance at the end is wonderful – He is with us. We never have to feel that we're working alone.

Healthy Bodies

Each of us has one body with many members,
and these members do not all have the same
function, so in Christ we who are many form one
body, and each member belongs to all the others.

Romans 12:4-5

A healthy body has many, many functioning parts. Some are visible to the observing eye and some are not. But each part is important to the ongoing health of the body and its proper functioning.

So it is with the local church body. God places different people with different gifts in each body. Each person must do their job or the body will not be healthy.

In order for souls to be won to Christ, each of us must do our job. We're all on the same team, reaching for the same goal. So we must work together.

Active Love

"I was hungry and you gave me something
to eat, I was thirsty and you gave me something
to drink, I was a stranger and you invited me in."

Matthew 25:35

Jesus said if we meet the physical needs of those around us, it's the same as meeting those needs for Him.

When you come across a person who does not have warm clothes or any food to eat, what do you do? Do you pat her on the back and say, "I'll pray for you," or do you find some way to give her food and clothing, then pray with her, thanking God for providing?

What good is it to share words about God's love with someone who is too hungry or in too much pain to listen? Show God's love, then tell about it.

The Light

"You are the light of the world. A city on a hill cannot be hidden. Neither do people light a lamp and put it under a bowl ... in the same way, let your light shine before men, that they may see your good deeds and praise your Father in heaven."

Matthew 5:14-16

Have you ever been in such total darkness that you could not see your hand in front of your face? It's kind of a scary place to be.

But when the tiniest glimmer of light comes in, it's such a good feeling. It seems to bring hope. That's the kind of responsibility you have, as Christ's ambassador in the world.

Your life that shines with His love and values is a light in a dark world. Those who are burdened by life and who have no hope, will see the light and be drawn to it.

Instruction Manual

All Scripture is God-breathed and is useful
for teaching, rebuking, correcting and
training in righteousness, so that the man of God
may be thoroughly equipped for every good work.

2 Timothy 3:16-17

Every job is easier if you have an instruction manual. Programming the DVD player is a piece of cake ... if you read the instructions.

God's work is easier, too, with the instruction manual He has provided. God's Word, the Bible, teaches us, corrects us, challenges us, and trains us to do any work He gives us to do.

Even the privilege of sharing His love with others is made easier by knowing His Word. Don't go into your work ill-equipped. Know His Word and let God use it in your life.

Lighthouse

For this is what the Lord has commanded us:
"I have made you a light for the Gentiles, that
you may bring salvation to the ends of the earth."

Acts 13:47

The interesting thing about doing God's work on earth is that it will never be finished. As long as we are alive, God has a job for us to do.

God doesn't want any people to miss the chance to know the joy of salvation. We have been entrusted with that message and it is both our privilege and our responsibility to share it.

God has made each of us a light. Our light, proclaiming His love, can shine like a lighthouse for those who are trying to find their way through the storms of life.

Patience

The Lord is not slow in keeping his promise,
as some understand slowness. He is patient
with you, not wanting anyone to perish,
but everyone to come to repentance.

2 Peter 3:9

Do you sometimes look at the mess our world is in and wonder why Christ doesn't just come back and end the horrific things? Why doesn't He put a stop to senseless wars, child abuse, murders and all the other things that make life so dangerous?

He could. He could come at any moment. He's not slow in returning as some might think.

God, in His incredible love and patience, doesn't want anyone to miss out on salvation. All people have the freedom to choose Him or not. He's hoping that all say yes. But they can't say yes if they haven't heard. That's where we come in.

We are to share the story of salvation every chance we get.

Eternal Security

"My sheep listen to my voice; I know them,
and they follow me. I give them eternal
life, and they shall never perish;
no one can snatch them out of my hand."

John 10:27-28

Eternal life. Never perish. These are two powerful phrases found in these verses. They are the reasons we should be sharing the gospel message every single chance we get.

Is the reality of eternity fixed in your mind? Do you believe there is a hell where people who do not know Christ will actually perish – with no reprieve?

When that reality looms in your mind, you will be moved to actively and eagerly tell people of God's love. Jesus promised that none of His sheep would perish. His sheep know His voice and follow Him. Following Him keeps us safe – forever.

Eager Sharing

The woman went back to the town and said
to the people, "Come, see a man who told me
everything I did. Could this be the Messiah?" ...
Many of the Samaritans from that town believed
in him because of the woman's testimony.

John 4:28-29, 39

The woman at the well met Jesus quite unexpectedly.
She was an outcast in society, not the kind of person
you would expect to turn into an avid missionary.
But as she talked with Jesus and the reality of who He
was began to sink into her heart, she couldn't keep
quiet about Him. She raced back to town and told
everyone about Him.

She had found something in Him that she wanted
others to know about. She apparently shared without
inhibitions and because of her, many people came to
Christ that day. She is a good example for us.

Jesus' Work

"The Son of Man came to seek
and save what was lost."

Luke 19:10

Jesus knew His purpose. He had a reason to walk this earth. He was part of a plan to restore life to mankind; to give people the opportunity to know God and to share in His heaven.

Every one of Jesus' actions, every word He spoke, was with this purpose in mind. In fact, He spoke these words because a sinful man named Zacchaeus had repented of his sin.

Jesus trained His disciples to carry on His work when He had gone back to heaven. We benefit from that training by reading the Bible and learning what Jesus taught.

We are to continue the work of bringing the message of God's love to a lost world. Jesus doesn't want any people to perish.

The Message of Hope

Jesus said to her, "I am the resurrection and
the life. He who believes in me will live,
even though he dies; and whoever
lives and believes in me will never die."

John 11:25-26

Here is the heart of our message for the world. Jesus offers eternal life to those who believe in Him. He came to earth, died for our sins and was resurrected. Now we who believe in Him can live forever with Him in heaven.

This is the heart of the message we have to share with a lost world. It's the hope of our salvation. All people on earth will die eventually, everyone knows that, but there is no reason to die without hope.

It is possible to know that heaven is sure and eternity can be spent there. Share the message, people are waiting to hear it.

Time Is Short

"I tell you, open your eyes and look at the fields! They are ripe for harvest. Even now the reaper draws his wages, even now he harvests the crop for eternal life so that the sower and the reaper may be glad together."

John 4:35-36

The fields are ready for harvest. God knows that people, many people, are ready to hear the salvation message. They are ready to accept Christ, but they have to hear the message.

It must make Him sad that some of those He has appointed to sow the seed are not doing the job.

Each of us has a role to play in bringing others to Christ. You may sow, you may water, you may reap. Whatever your job is, get busy and do it. Time is short.

Working Out His Plan

He who began a good work in you will carry
it on to completion until the day of Christ Jesus.

Philippians 1:6

Are you experiencing a time when it seems like everything is going wrong and problems are piling one on top of the other? It's hard not to get discouraged during these times.

Paul reminds you that God has not forgotten you – even during the tough times of life. God's work in your life is not cursory. He doesn't get tired or busy with other things and forget about you. He has a plan for you and will continue working out that plan all of your life.

So, in the depths of discouragement, try to remember that the things happening to you are not outside of God's knowledge. Lean on Him, call on Him and trust Him.

Support Base

Cast all your anxiety on
him because he cares for you.

1 Peter 5:7

Imagine a strength so powerful that you can pour all your fears, pain, problems, insecurities and anxieties into it and know they will be handled ... forever. That's God's love. He invites you to bring all of those things to Him and leave them at the foot of the cross.

He will comfort you, strengthen you and encourage you because He cares about you. His care was shown in a very real way when Christ voluntarily came to earth to show, by example, how to live with others and for God.

He took your sin on Himself when He died on the cross and now He lives in heaven, making intercession for you. He knows what life on earth is like and He's willing to help you through it. Just ask Him.

Bodyguards

He will command his angels concerning
you to guard you in all your ways; they
will lift you up in their hands, so that you
will not strike your foot against a stone.

Psalm 91:11-12

One of the worst things about discouragement is that
you often feel as if no one truly understands what
you're going through.

Sometimes you may even sense that your family
and friends are tired of hearing about your problems
and are beginning to avoid you. You can end up feeling
very alone in your struggles.

Well, you're not. Nothing that happens to you
surprises God. He knows when you need extra strength
and protection and He has appointed guardians to
take care of His children.

You may not even know what you have been
protected from ... but rest assured that you
are not alone.

Crossing Guard

Even though I walk through the valley of the shadow of death, I will fear no evil, for you are with me; your rod and your staff, they comfort me.

Psalm 23:4

If you've ever lost a loved one to death or faced death yourself, you may have found comfort in this verse.

Death can bring a fear of the unknown ... the crossing from this life to the next. We know, however, that we will not be alone as we cross from this life to the next. God will be with us. His rod and staff will guide us and protect us even in the valley of the shadow of death.

There are certainly unknowns about death and the afterlife, but the things we do know assure us that we won't be alone on that journey.

A Hiding Place

The LORD is good, a refuge in times of
trouble. He cares for those who trust in him.

Nahum 1:7

A refuge. That's what we all want, isn't it? When the burdens of life weigh down on us and we can't find relief, we just want to run away and hide.

What is a refuge? A safe place. A protected place. A hiding place. God is available to be all those things to us in our times of discouragement.

But the second sentence of this verse is very important. He's available for those who trust in Him. Trust is an interesting thing because it means believing God is there and that He's working, even when you can't actually see what He's doing.

Trust Him to take care of you and those you love, then He will truly be your refuge.

Amazing Love

How great is the love the Father has lavished on us, that we should be called children of God!

1 John 3:1

Parent/child relationships are sometimes difficult. Often, parents want to do everything for their children, from giving them whatever they can to solving all their problems for them.

However, good parents know that sometimes children have to go through difficult times in order to learn valuable lessons and children simply can't have everything they want. It wouldn't be good for them. That shows that the parent really loves the child.

You are God's child and He showers you with His love – that doesn't mean He gives you everything you think you need. But if you stop and think about all He does for you, and all He does give you, you will know that you are totally, completely loved.

Fighting Discouragement

A heart at peace gives life to
the body, but envy rots the bones.

Proverbs 14:30

Why do you struggle with discouragement? What is it that gets you down? Are you looking around at friends and seeing that they have bigger houses, nicer cars, more impressive careers and more successful children? Do you find yourself longing for some of the things your friends have? If so, you're setting yourself up for discouragement.

A heart at peace is content (of course it aspires to continue to grow and improve) and does not envy others. Being at peace actually assists the growing/improving process because you can achieve more when you're not discouraged or frantically racing around trying to grab more out of life.

Let your heart be at peace and defeat discouragement. You'll be glad you did.

Power Living

I pray also that the eyes of your heart may be
enlightened in order that you may know the hope
to which he has called you, the riches of his
glorious inheritance in the saints, and his
incomparably great power for us who believe.

Ephesians 1:18-19

In our discouragement, we sometimes get stuck in
tunnel vision. All we can see before us are the things
that are wrong in our lives. We know we don't have
the power to change those things ... they are simply
out of our hands. So we get discouraged.

Paul's prayer for the Ephesians has a message for us,
too. Pray that the eyes of your heart will be opened
to the inheritance you have as God's child.

Remember how God has worked on your behalf
in the past and that His power, His great power is
available to you today.

Breaking the Cycle

Praise the LORD, O my soul, and forget not all his
benefits – who forgives all your sins and heals
all your diseases, who redeems your life from
the pit and crowns you with love and compassion,
who satisfies your desires with good things
so that your youth is renewed like the eagle's.

Psalm 103:2-4

"God, do this. Fix that. Guide me, show me, help me."
Does your discouragement stem from what God
doesn't do? Do you make plans for your life, ask Him
to bless them, then get discouraged because He
doesn't do what you want Him to do?

The psalmist encourages you to remember what
God does for you every day. Read through this list,
stop and meditate on each of God's loving acts. When
your mind is filled with these good memories, perhaps
the discouragement cycle will break as you praise
and love God.

Memories

The LORD your God has blessed you in all
the work of your hands. He has watched
over your journey through this vast desert.
These forty years the LORD your God has been
with you, and you have not lacked anything.

Deuteronomy 2:7

Moses spoke these words to the Hebrews to remind
them of God's miraculous works on their behalf. The
Hebrews had a habit of quickly forgetting God's work
and sliding back into their pattern of complaining
about their situation – they got discouraged. Moses
knew it would help them to focus on God's goodness
and care.

If you're struggling with discouragement, why not
try Moses' remedy? Step back and remember how
God has blessed you and cared for you. Has He let you
lack for anything? Has He blessed your work? Hold
on to those things and move forward trusting Him.

Rest for the Weary

"Come to me, all you who are weary
and burdened, and I will give you rest."

Matthew 11:28

What an offer this is! Jesus offers us a respite from the heavy load of discouragement. Close your eyes and imagine Him standing before you, arms outstretched, beckoning you to come to Him. You walk toward Him and with each step you can feel the weight lifting from your shoulders. It's a good mental picture, isn't it?

Jesus especially calls those who are worn out from carrying heavy burdens. He knows that they most need what He has to offer.

Perhaps you are one whom He is calling. Are you ready to take the first step toward Him? The promise of rest is pretty enticing, isn't it? Let go of your discouragement and go to Him. You'll be glad you did.

Never Alone

The LORD upholds all those who
fall and lifts up all who are bowed down.

Psalm 145:14

What do you want most when you're discouraged? Relief from the discouragement? The knowledge that someone cares about you? Where do you turn to find this?

If you are searching for it from friends or loved ones, you may be disappointed. The empathy of other people can only go so far.

But if you take your pain and discouragement to the Lord, stay quiet before Him, and wait for Him, you will find what you're looking for. He is the only One who can truly lift you up. He loves you very much. He cares about the heavy load you're carrying. He may not take your problems away, but He will walk with you through them.

You are not alone. Go to Him, wait quietly before Him, sense His love.

Obey Always

Be strong and very courageous. Be careful
to obey all the law my servant Moses gave you;
do not turn from it to the right or to the left,
that you may be successful wherever you go.

Joshua 1:7

God's people have no reason to be defeated or
discouraged. His power and strength are available to
us. His command to Joshua in this verse is repeated
three times in the first chapter of Joshua. *Be strong
and courageous.*

What can defeat you when God is working for you?
But there is a stipulation in this verse, too. Be careful
to obey – all the time – to the best of your ability.

If you're discouraged about failures in your life, stop
and consider whether or not you've been obedient
to God's laws. Don't expect God to bless you if you
aren't obeying Him to the fullest extent of your
knowledge and ability.

Rumble or Humble

Humble yourselves, therefore, under God's
mighty hand, that he may lift you up in due time.

1 Peter 5:6

Arrogance and pride will get you nowhere. If you approach life thinking that you know best and that you've got things under control, you're going to have major problems.

People who live that way tell God, "Hey, I'll call you if I need you, otherwise ... hands off!" Well, that, my friends, is not what God wants to hear.

What does it mean to humble yourself before God? It means letting go of the controls, bowing your head and heart before Him and waiting for His leading and direction. So, acknowledge that God is guiding and leading you. You can trust Him. If you humble yourself before Him, He will lift you up. You will know that you're in good hands.

Learn and Grow

We know that in all things God works
for the good of those who love him, who
have been called according to his purpose.

Romans 8:28

When you're stuck in discouragement it's hard to imagine that anything good can come from what you're going through. Sometimes it's even hard to imagine that God would allow these things to happen.

This verse is sometimes misquoted or at least misinterpreted. It doesn't say that God makes bad things good. It does say that in all situations He works *for* the good. There are lessons to be learned and character qualities to be developed in each situation.

If you love Him and are obeying Him, then ask Him to work for good in your difficult situation. Learn and grow from it. Make it count for something. You'll be a better person and a stronger child of God for it.

The Great Physician

He heals the brokenhearted
and binds up their wounds.

Psalm 147:3

The universe is so big. There are so many crisis situations. There are so many people with serious problems. Do you sometimes feel as if your measly little problems couldn't possibly be that important to God?

At the same time, though, you just want to matter to Him, right? You just want to know that He cares about you and what you're going through. He does.

Read through the Psalms and you will find verses like this one over and over. God cares about you. He cares when you're hurting. He will help you. He will mend your broken heart. He will bandage your wounds. He will help you move forward.

The Big Picture

"Do not let your hearts be troubled. Trust in God;
trust also in me. In my Father's house are many
rooms: if it were not so, I would have told you.
I am going there to prepare a place for you."

John 14:1-2

Discouragement makes you focus on the moment. You get stuck on the pain, the hopelessness or the loneliness in your heart. You can't seem to see a light at the end of the tunnel or if you do, you fear it's a train rushing toward you.

Trust becomes a lost element of your walk with God. There's no future in that. Allow God to remind you that the hard times won't last forever. He has an incredible future planned for you.

If He's gone to all that trouble to plan eternity, He's going to take care of today, too. Trust Him.

Precious

For he will deliver the needy who cry out, the afflicted who have no one to help. He will take pity on the weak and the needy and save the needy from death. He will rescue them from oppression and violence, for precious is their blood in his sight.

Psalm 72:12-14

If you skim through this verse you'll miss a very important word – precious. Imagine being precious to the Creator! You are.

At one time or another we have all been aware of the conditions mentioned here in our lives. This verse affirms that each of us is precious to God. He cares whether even a single drop of your blood is spilled. Your life is precious to Him.

Savor that thought for a minute. The almighty God, who has the weight of the world shouting for His attention, thinks you are precious. Makes you feel pretty special, doesn't it?

Blessings

"Blessed are the poor in spirit, for theirs
is the kingdom of heaven. Blessed are
those who mourn, for they will be comforted."

Matthew 5:3-4

Does it seem to you that the strong, powerful people of the world are the ones who succeed in life? They seem to be in positions of authority, and have influence over others. They set the standard for the rest of us.

But Jesus said in the Beatitudes that in the big picture the humble and meek will be blessed. Those who mourn loved ones will be comforted. Jesus preferred to spend time with the not-so-powerful, the not-so-influential people of His world.

He knew that those who were hurting would seek Him out more readily than those who felt self-sufficient. So, if you're hurting today, turn to Jesus. He promised you comfort, blessings and the hope of heaven.

Dark Nights

No one will be able to stand up against you all
the days of your life. As I was with Moses, so I will
be with you; I will never leave you nor forsake you.

Joshua 1:5

Do you have trouble sleeping when something is
weighing on your mind? Do you find yourself pacing
the floor half the night, unable to quiet your racing
mind? If so, you know how dark the night gets just
before dawn. In that quiet dark you can feel so alone
with your problems.

Just as God promised to be with Joshua all the
days of his life, He is with you. He promises to never
leave you or forsake you.

Even if at this moment you can't sense His presence,
be assured that God is with you. He knows what you're
going through and He cares.

Behind the Scenes

He is the image of the invisible God, the
firstborn over all creation. For by him all
things were created: things in heaven and on
earth, visible and invisible, whether thrones or
powers or rulers or authorities; all things were
created by him and for him. He is before
all things, and in him all things hold together.

Colossians 1:15-17

Christ is the image of God Himself. He was before
all things and He is what holds all things together.
Christ was involved in the creation of all things and
all earthly powers.

Why are we reviewing these well-known facts, you
ask? Because Christ who has all power, knowledge
and wisdom can take care of you.

Whatever is knocking you down is not too big for
Him. Take your problems to Him, rest in Him. You
don't have to worry about things anymore.
Trust Him to take care of you.

The Great Comforter

Praise be to the God and Father of our
Lord Jesus Christ, the Father of compassion
and the God of all comfort, who comforts
us in all our troubles, so that we can
comfort those in any trouble with the comfort
we ourselves have received from God.

2 Corinthians 1:3-4

Being a child of God doesn't mean you won't have difficult times in life. He does, however, walk with us through the hard times. Frankly, He loves you so much that He hurts when you hurt. Because of that compassion, He promises to comfort you when your heart is breaking.

How does God show comfort? Sometimes through people in your life, sometimes through a sense deep in your soul that He loves you. When you experience God's comfort, you can show comfort and compassion to others – bring God's comfort to them.

Victory!

The LORD said to Joshua, "Do not be afraid
of them; I have given them into your hand.
Not one of them will be able to withstand you."

Joshua 10:8

Sometimes it feels as if life is out of control. Things happen so quickly that you can't grab on anywhere. A familiar panic begins to grow in your stomach and color every moment of every day.

Perhaps you are afraid that no one is really in control. Perhaps it seems that the bad guys are winning.

Well, in the long run the bad guys will not win. God told Joshua that he shouldn't be afraid and you also have the assurance that in the final chapter, God is the victor, and you're on His team.

So, whatever weighs on you today, you have nothing to fear. You're already assured of victory.

Certainty

He who avenges blood remembers;
he does not ignore the cry of the afflicted.

Psalm 9:12

As you read through the psalms you hear the psalmist's cry to God over and over again. He questions why God is silent, why He doesn't seem to hear or to answer the heartfelt cries of the writer.

Do you feel like that sometimes? You pour out your heart to God, begging to hear His voice and know His response to your prayer and it seems that all you hear is ... silence.

That's hard, isn't it? In this psalm of praise David reminds you to praise God because He does hear your prayers. He does remember you and care about what you're going through.

In His time He *will* answer. You can know that for certain as you wait on Him.

Future Joy

The ransomed of the LORD will return. They
will enter Zion with singing; everlasting joy will
crown their heads. Gladness and joy will overtake
them, and sorrow and sighing will flee away.

Isaiah 35:10

In this description of the victorious return of God's
people to Jerusalem, we read of exuberant and
overwhelming joy.

Have you ever been so filled with joy that you are
overcome and you can't find words to express yourself?

The joy of the Israelites mentioned here is just a
hint of the joy ahead for you. God has delivered you
from the bondage of sin and the joy of heaven awaits.
The sorrow and sighing that fills your heart now will
end one day.

You will be overwhelmed with gladness and joy
tomorrow and the pain and discouragement of
today will be forgotten.

Hanging in There

Blessed is the man who perseveres under
trial, because when he has stood the test,
he will receive the crown of life that
God has promised to those who love him.

James 1:12

When you're in the middle of a trial, the last thing
you want to hear about is the joy of persevering ...
hanging in there. When you're hurting, you just want
the hurt to stop, right?

The reality is that very few people make it through
life without times of discouragement, stress and pain.
It's going to happen. The key is what you do when it
does. You can cave in and become a sniveling, whining,
defeated woman, or you can persevere. That means
you keep on going, keep your chin up, don't give up.

Doing so results in a prize you could never have
imagined – the crown of life – God's reward for your
perseverance.

How Do You Spell Relief?

When my spirit grows faint within
me, it is you who know my way.

Psalm 142:3

David wrote this psalm from a cave where he was hiding from those who wanted to kill him. Life doesn't get much more stressful than that. We can learn quite a lesson from David. In this stressful, discouraging time of his life, he knew that God was in control.

David didn't deserve to be hunted down, he had done nothing wrong. He had been anointed to be King of Israel. He was God's choice, but at the moment things weren't going well.

David didn't give up and get angry with God. He continually cried out to God for help. He knew that the answer to his problems was in God's hands. That's a good thing to remember.

Get Moving!

See, the LORD your God has given you
the land. Go up and take possession of it
as the LORD, the God of your fathers, told
you. Do not be afraid; do not be discouraged.

Deuteronomy 1:21

Is it possible that your discouragement comes from lack of action? Perhaps you know something you are supposed to be doing – a friend you should witness to, a job you should take, a ministry you should get involved in, a habit you should break – something that requires you to take action; but you don't.

For whatever reason, you haven't gotten off the couch and done a thing. Well, if you know that to be true in your life, don't go complaining to God about your discouragement. Show your trust in Him.

Get up and "take the land God has given you." Put work gloves on your faith and get busy.

Big Picture

"I have loved you with an everlasting love;
I have drawn you with loving-kindness."

Jeremiah 31:3

We frail human beings get caught up in the moment.
When we get so busy we can't sit or sleep or rest at all,
when the burdens of life pile up on us and we can't
see daylight, we forget the big picture.

What is the big picture, you ask? Simple – God loves
us and draws us to Himself with incredible kindness.
It's not a bad idea to remember that everything that
happens to us in this life is simply a training ground
for eternity, and eternity is what counts.

So, step back from your problems and remember
that God loves you. There is more to life than the
burdens you're struggling with right now.

Mind Food

Finally, brothers, whatever is true, whatever
is noble, whatever is right, whatever is pure,
whatever is lovely, whatever is admirable –
if anything is excellent or praiseworthy –
think about such things.

Philippians 4:8

Garbage in, garbage out. What does that mean?
Well, if you fill your physical body with junk food, it
will become overweight and not very healthy. In the
same way, if you fill your mind with negative, unkind,
impure thoughts, it will show in your attitude and
the way you treat other people.

Fill your mind with true, noble, right, pure, lovely
and admirable things and your attitude will be more
positive, your energy levels will be higher, you will be
more hopeful about life itself.

Where do you find these good things? In God's
Word. Read it, absorb it and implant it in your mind.
Let His Word guide your thoughts.

The Place to Start

Search me, O God, and know my heart;
test me and know my anxious thoughts.
See if there is any offensive way
in me, and lead me in the way everlasting.

Psalm 139:23-24

Discouragement happens and you just want it to stop. You can try all the positive thinking you want, you can try every formula for overcoming discouragement outlined in women's magazines, you can eat every chocolate bar within ten miles ... and still be discouraged.

A better place to begin the battle is found in this verse. Prayer. Allow God to search your heart, with nothing held back. Allow Him to show you what is below the surface, beneath the fine Christian veneer you wear for all to see.

Ask God to reveal the sin in your heart, ask Him to lead you away from it. He will, and you'll be the better for it.

Back-Up

When I called, you answered me;
you made me bold and stouthearted.

Psalm 138:3

"I'm calling for back-up!" TV show cops often announce that to the bad guys, and the bad guys shake in their boots. They know they are done for because the back-up guarantees they will be caught. The ability to call for back-up gives the single police officer courage because he knows he isn't alone in this situation. He has help to do his work.

When you turn to God and cry out for His help, you can be encouraged and strengthened by the knowledge that you have back-up. You aren't alone in your struggles. He will answer you with His guidance and awareness of His love.

That should give you courage and determination in whatever is before you.

Follow-Through

This is the confidence we have in approaching
God: that if we ask anything according
to his will, he hears us. And if we know
that he hears us – whatever we ask – we
know that we have what we asked of him.

1 John 5:14-15

Teenagers are not always the most dependable in seeing things through – at least things their parents ask them. A simple request such as, "Could you put the trash out for pick up?" will usually result in "Yeah." But somehow it just doesn't happen. The teen's intentions were good ... but things got in the way of his follow-through.

We never have to worry about lack of follow-through from God. When we talk to Him, He hears us and when we make requests of Him, according to His will, and in obedience to Him, He will follow through in helping us. He promised.

Strong Foundation

Look to the LORD and his
strength; seek his face always.

1 Chronicles 16:11

Where do you turn when you need strength or help? Some people turn to substances – drugs, tranquilizers, alcohol, or food. Some people turn to friends. Friends encourage us in life and sometimes God uses them to guide us. But the best place we should turn – the first place to turn – is to God.

He is dependable and constant. His motives are always pure – to help us become more obedient and to grow in our service to Him. While others may have more selfish goals or may waver in their support of us, God's strength is a foundation of rock beneath us.

Our goal should be to constantly be looking to Him, seeking His face for our guidance, encouragement, and strength.

Generous Giver

"Ask and it will be given to you; seek and you will
find; knock and the door will be opened to you.
For everyone who asks receives; he who seeks finds;
and to him who knocks the door will be opened."

Matthew 7:7-8

The look of sheer joy on a child's face when she tears
open a package and finds exactly what she wanted
delights a parent's heart. When you love someone,
you enjoy doing things for them and giving them gifts
and helping them. When someone you care about has
a need, all they have to do is ask and you will quickly
go to their aid.

God wants to help you, too. It's important to
recognize your need for Him and your dependence
on Him. When you turn to Him and admit your need
for help, guidance and wisdom, He'll be there. You
can count on it.

Giving Credit

Help us, O God our Savior, for the
glory of your name; deliver us and
forgive our sins for your name's sake.

Psalm 79:9

The best way to ensure that coworkers, friends or
family will not want to help you with anything is to
take personal credit for when they do assist you –
and completely ignore any contribution they made.
It's no fun to be taken for granted or to be ignored.

Keep that in mind when asking God for help. When
you plead for His guidance, protection or intervention
in your life and He gives it, give Him the credit.

Use His answers to prayer as an opportunity to
praise Him. Then people around you will see the
evidence of His personal involvement in your life. It
will be a testament to His love.

Spreading the Good News

Pray for us that the message of
the Lord may spread rapidly and
be honored, just as it was with you.

2 Thessalonians 3:1

Good news spreads quickly. When a college girl gets engaged, it's not long before the entire dorm hears the news and rush to see the ring. The message of God's love should spread even more quickly.

The apostle Paul felt that urgency. He wanted it to flow like a rushing river. He believed that prayer was vital to sharing the gospel successfully.

Remember to support your pastor, Sunday school teachers and missionaries in their efforts to spread the good news. Request prayer from your circle of supporters so that you will be able to share the gospel with people you meet.

Help Me!

Immediately the boy's father exclaimed,
"I do believe; help me overcome my unbelief!"

Mark 9:24

This is a powerful, honest prayer. No matter how long we've known the Lord, there is always room for our faith to grow stronger.

We run up against situations when our faith may falter and we can't seem to connect with God. Deep inside we know that we do believe; we just can't understand how the belief fits our current need.

The bottom line is that our faith is not negotiable. But we recognize that because of a certain crisis, our faith needs to grow. It's okay to admit that to God and to cry out in prayer, as this heartbroken father did, asking God to help your unbelief turn to belief. He will honor your honesty and answer your prayer.

Pray for Guidance

Teach me to do your will, for you are my God;
may your good Spirit lead me on level ground.

Psalm 143:10

Christianity isn't just about accepting Christ so your eternal destiny is settled; it's also about learning how to live your life.

God created people to live in community with others. Others may come to Him because they see His love in you. God will help you learn to live in love with others. His Word is your guidebook for learning how to relate to Him and to other people.

Your efforts to learn how God wants you to serve Him are fruitless unless you ask Him to teach you. Ask God to teach you His will for you – it's always a work in progress – changing and growing.

Make sure all your efforts to know His will are bathed in prayer for His guidance.

Praise!

Praise the LORD. Praise God in his sanctuary;
praise him in his mighty heavens ... Let everything
that has breath praise the LORD. Praise the LORD.

Psalm 150:1, 6

"Give me ... I want ... give me, help me, give me."
How much of your time in prayer is spent in asking
God to do something, or help you with something?
Now think about how much of your prayers consist
of praise for who God is.

Is your prayer time so rushed that you feel you
must quickly get through your list of requests? Do
you take time to just meditate on who He is and His
creation, the evidence of His love for you; the gift of
His Word, the Bible?

There is so much to praise Him for. Decide to put
your requests at the end of your prayer time. Praise
Him first!

Power in Prayer

I urge, then, first of all, that requests,
prayers, intercession and thanksgiving be
made for everyone – for kings and those
in authority, that we may live peaceful
and quiet lives in all godliness and holiness.

1 Timothy 2:1-2

When a group of people get together it is not uncommon for some of them, for some of the time, to begin talking about politics and complaining about what the government is or isn't doing. This must have been common in Bible times, too, because Paul urged believers to pray for their leaders.

There is power in prayer and the way Christians can turn the world's attention toward God is by praying for the decisions our leaders make.

Paul urged us to remember our leaders. By lifting them up to God, praying about the influences on them, and asking God to give them wisdom and discernment, we influence our own quality of life.

No Worries

Do not be anxious about anything, but in everything, by prayer and petition, with thanksgiving, present your requests to God.

Philippians 4:6

It's the middle of the night. Darkness blankets the room. You should be sleeping, but you're wide awake. Your mind races with concerns about what could happen. You're living in a land of "what ifs".

Sound familiar? Unfortunately, many of us regularly visit What If Land. But it isn't necessary. Much of what we worry about is out of our hands. They are situations we can't change – but God can.

He invites us to bring our requests to Him. We can know that He will take care of things, because He tells us not to worry. So, don't waste your energy on worrying; use it to praise God, thank Him for His care, and give your worries to Him.

Private Prayer

"When you pray, go into your room,
close the door and pray to your Father
who is unseen. Then your Father, who
sees what is done in secret, will reward you."

Matthew 6:6

When you settle down to pray, does your mind wander? Do you find yourself praying some, then making a mental list of things you need to do?

This verse seems to have a dual purpose in teaching about prayer. We are not to publicly pray fancy prayers – just for show. We are also encouraged to withdraw from the busyness of our lives and concentrate as we pray.

Satan will try to disrupt your prayer time – that's a given. He may remind you to pick up the dry-cleaning or call your child's teacher – anything to pull your mind away from prayer. Don't do that! Give your full attention to God, shut out everything else. Enjoy God!

Just Ask

You do not have because you do not ask God.

James 4:2

There is an old expression that says, "You won't know if you don't ask." You won't know if another person will do something for you or give you something if you don't ask them.

The other person may not know the intensity of your desire or even know of your specific need until you ask them for help.

Prayer is the way we communicate our requests to God. Of course, He knows what we need before we even ask Him, but we may not really know until we formulate the words in our hearts.

Think about what you want God to do for you and what you want Him to teach you. Then, ask Him. He's waiting to help you.

Family Prayers

Pray in the Spirit on all occasions with all kinds of
prayers and requests. With this in mind, be alert
and always keep on praying for all the saints.

Ephesians 6:18

Belonging to a team or a family unit means you have
the support of the other members. Sometimes that
support is what keeps you going when you don't feel
that you can take another step.

You experience that same kind of support from
the family of God. Each of us should be in constant
prayer for one another, lifting up and encouraging
one another every day.

Be alert to those around you, sense their needs,
and constantly bring them before the Lord. They will
do the same thing for you – you can't fall too far, no
matter what happens, when you know your brothers
and sisters are holding you before the Lord. What
power!

Forgive
and Forget

"Forgive us our sins, for we also
forgive everyone who sins against us."

Luke 11:4

This verse comes straight from the example Jesus gave of the correct way to pray. He taught that it is important to ask God's forgiveness on a daily basis. It's tempting to scoot right over this in our prayer time and head right to the "meat" of our prayer, which is generally the requests we want God to hear and answer.

But why should He grant our requests if we aren't obeying Him? The tricky part is that none of us can obey all the time – that's beyond human capability. So, remember to calm your heart and mind as you begin praying, confess your sins and shortcomings and ask His forgiveness. Then ask for His strength to help you forgive those who have wronged you. Forgive and forget.

Praying for the World

Your prayers and gifts to the poor have come up as a memorial offering before God.

Acts 10:4

Are you a prayer snob? Do you pray only for your friends or family members or people who are, for the most part, just like you? Are you impatient with the less fortunate in the world? Particularly impatient with those who (you think) could work a bit harder to make their own lot in life better? If so ... shame on you!

Paul tells us in this verse that our concern through prayer and actual gifts to the poor is a pleasant offering to God. He is pleased when we are concerned enough about others, even other people groups, to pray for them and when we give to help their living situations improve.

We should lift up one another any way we can.

Praying in Belief

"Whatever you ask for in prayer, believe that you have received it, and it will be yours."

Mark 11:24

Trust the One to whom you pray. You can pray for hours and hours, using the fanciest five-dollar words you can think of, but if you don't believe that God hears your prayers and that He has the power and authority to answer them ... you're wasting your time and energy.

Proper praying begins with spending time in God's Word and aligning your will with His. That means you basically want the same things out of life. Then, when you pray, you can believe that God will answer you.

He's waiting to give you the desires of your heart. So, learn about Him, know Him, pray to Him and trust Him. You'll be glad you did!

Forgive and Pray

"When you stand praying, if you hold anything
against anyone, forgive him, so that your
Father in heaven may forgive you your sins."

Mark 11:25

Don't ask for something you aren't willing to give.
It's pointless to ask God to forgive your sins if you
are not willing to forgive someone who has wronged
you. No one goes through life without touching other
lives. You have to work with others and usually live
around others.

Once in a while, either on purpose or accidentally,
someone may wrong you. You can grab that wrong
and hold on to it. You can nurse it until it grows to a
big wrong in your mind. But if you're going to do that,
how could you dare to ask God to forgive your sins?

Be willing to show the same kind of grace to others
that you want God to show to you.

Power!

The prayer of a righteous
person is powerful and effective.

James 5:16

"I wish there was something I could do." Do you
sometimes think that when you see someone suffer-
ing or experiencing a difficult time?

Well there is something you can do. Pray. Prayer
makes a difference. God promises that our prayers are
powerful and effective. However, there is one word
in James 5:16 that cannot be overlooked – righteous.
It's important when we come before God to confess
our sins and ask forgiveness. Then we stand before
Him clean and righteous. It's also important to live
our lives in obedience to Him.

We can't do what we want, then expect Him to
do what we want Him to do. Live as righteously as
possible, confess your sins, then pray with all your
heart. It makes a difference.

When You Can't Pray

We do not know what we ought to pray for,
but the Spirit himself intercedes for us with
groans that words cannot express. And he
who searches our hearts knows the mind
of the Spirit, because the Spirit intercedes
for the saints in accordance with God's will.

Romans 8:26-27

Sometimes the pain is so deep that we can't even
pray. We want God to make the pain stop – heal the
disease – repair the relationship – restore the job. But
deep down inside we know that may not be what God
wants – and so we don't know what to pray.

When our hearts are at a loss for the right words
the Spirit takes over. He lives within our hearts and
He cries out to God for us. So, when you can't find
the words, be comforted that the Holy Spirit
is interceding for you, and God hears His
prayers.

Love One Another

"May they be brought to complete unity to let the world know that you sent me and have loved them even as you have loved me."

John 17:23

Jesus prayed for us ... His followers. He wanted us to live in unity – to get along. He knew that non-believers would be drawn to us and to Him by the love they see in our lives. How can we tell them about God's love for them if they see us fighting and scrapping with our Christian brothers and sisters? Nearly every church experiences times when the members don't get along.

Sometimes the struggles between denominations become public. That must make Satan smile. Join Jesus in praying for unity among believers ... even across denominational lines. Pray that we will stand strong together, as evidence of His love for the entire world.

Being Teachable

Show me your ways, O LORD, teach me your paths;
guide me in your truth and teach me, for you are
God, my Savior, and my hope is in you all day long.

Psalm 25:4-5

With a baby's first steps, a whole new world opens up to explore, with many lessons to be learned. It's the same for believers as we learn to live the Christian life.

The foundation for those lessons is to be on our knees, when we ask the Lord to show us how to live and what path to follow in life.

A key part of this is found at the end of verse 5 – *all day long*. It's important to patiently wait for God's guidance instead of plowing ahead in life.

We must be quiet before Him ... for a while ... to let our minds and hearts settle down and hear His guidance.

Fully Equipped

May the God of peace ... equip you with
everything good for doing his will, and may he
work in us what is pleasing to him, through Jesus
Christ, to whom be glory for ever and ever. Amen.

Hebrews 13:20-21

"I can't do it, God!" "This is too hard." "I don't know
how!" Have you ever felt like this? God will give you
the words, actions, thoughts, and abilities you need
to do the work He gives you to do. He doesn't send
you into the world unequipped.

Pray for yourself and for others, asking God to give
you all you need to do His work.

Don't minimize the skills and talents He gives,
just remember to give the glory to Jesus Christ for
any gifts God gives you, and get busy doing His work!

Always Special!

Keep me as the apple of your eye;
hide me in the shadow of your wings.

Psalm 17:8

The "apple of your eye" presents kind of an unusual mental image, doesn't it? When someone is the apple of your eye, it means they are special and precious to you. You delight in them.

The wonderful thing about the psalmist's words is that they confirm that you are the apple of God's eye – you're special to Him! So special that He will hide you under His wings just as a mother hen gathers her chicks under her wings, hiding them from view and protecting them from any dangers.

Run to Him, trusting in His concern and love for you and allow Him to protect you from the cares of the world.

First Step

Then I acknowledged my sin to you and
did not cover up my iniquity, I said, "I
will confess my transgressions to the LORD" –
and you forgave the guilt of my sin.

Psalm 32:5

Electric currents rush through wires to light your home, make your radio or TV play ... unless there is a break in the wires. If anything blocks the lines, the power is broken.

Your relationship with the Lord is like this, too. Before you come to Him with praise for who He is, His power, His love and strength ... before you bring your requests to Him, asking His intervention and help ... before you speak any other words to Him – confess.

Admit your own shortcomings and sins and ask His forgiveness. Then you can come to Him, cleansed by the blood of Jesus, pure in the sight of God.

Confess then Praise

Praise the LORD, O my soul; all my
inmost being, praise his holy name.

Psalm 103:1

It feels good to hear someone say nice things about you, doesn't it? It lifts your spirits, encourages you and gives you confidence.

Now, God doesn't need our encouragement or affirmation, but He does delight in our praise. Why? Because as we praise Him, we focus on His character and attributes. Taking time in our prayer life to think about the power, awesomeness, compassion and love of God results in our praise of Him and that encourages us.

Strange, isn't it? We give Him praise and we end up feeling closer and more loving to Him because we remember how wonderful He is.

So, after you've confessed your sin to Him, praise Him for all that He is!

Powerful Faith

"If you have faith and do not doubt ... you can say to this mountain, 'Go throw yourself into the sea, and it will be done. If you believe, you will receive whatever you ask for in prayer.'"

Matthew 21:21-22

Is your faith strong? Think about this – scientists say that we use only a miniscule portion of our brains. If we could figure out how to harness the potential of our brains, there is no telling what we could achieve.

This is even more true of our faith. Our prayers could be so powerful that a mountain would throw itself into the sea if only our faith were strong enough.

Bring your requests to God, and as you do ask Him to help your faith grow and grow. There is no limit to what praying in real faith can accomplish!

Urgent Need

"The harvest is plentiful but the workers
are few. Ask the Lord of the harvest, therefore,
to send out workers into his harvest field."

Matthew 9:37-38

Hell is a real place. There are people in this world right now who will spend eternity in hell. Sometimes that truth gets muddled up and lost in our concept of a loving God. God is loving, but He has laid out the guidelines for entering His heaven and He isn't going to change His mind.

We should sense His urgency to spread the gospel to the entire world. Perhaps God hasn't called you to go to a foreign country ... but you can pray.

Pray that God will call workers to spread the Good News. Pray that those whom He calls will answer that call. Pray with urgency.

Scripture Prayers

Let the word of Christ dwell in you richly as you teach and admonish one another with all wisdom, and as you sing psalms, hymns and spiritual songs with gratitude in your hearts to God.

Colossians 3:16

Pray the words of Scripture. What better way to gain understanding of God's Word than to memorize it and pray it back to God. As you do this, He will open your heart to the possibilities of knowing Him and absorbing His Words into your heart.

You can pray God's promises to Him because they are just that – promises He gives you as to how He wants to work in your heart and life. You can be assured that you are praying in His will when you are praying God's own words.

Spend time reading and learning His Word, then joyfully pray in God's own words!

Prayer for Growth

May my cry come before you, O LORD;
give me understanding according to your word.

Psalm 119:169

It's so much fun to watch a child discover the world around her. Blowing the fuzzies of a dandelion, playing with a puppy, watching fish swim ... the joy of discovery is part of growing up.

We should know the same kind of joy as our relationship with God grows. We should never feel that we know all there is to know about God; we understand Scripture as much as we ever will; we walk in faith as much as possible. It's just not true.

Ask God ... no, *cry out* to God to increase your understanding and grow your faith. Don't ever be content with your Christian walk – strive to grow closer and closer to Him!

Grasping the Love

I pray that you, being rooted and established
in love, may have power, together with all
the saints, to grasp how wide and long
and high and deep is the love of Christ.

Ephesians 3:17-18

It is virtually impossible to trust someone whom you don't love. You will constantly be questioning motives if you don't believe you are loved, too. That's why Paul prayed that the Christians in Ephesus would understand the depths of God's love.

This understanding comes through the Holy Spirit and it is foundational to trusting God. Grasping the extent of God's love lays the groundwork for you to trust Him.

You know that someone who loves you that much wants the very best for you. Pray that God will begin to allow you to understand the depths of His love and to help that understanding grow ever deeper.

Tug-of-War

Trust in the LORD and do good; dwell in the land
and enjoy safe pasture. Delight yourself in the
LORD and he will give you the desires of your heart.

Psalm 37:3-4

Have you ever played tug-of-war? You and your
teammates hold a rope and pull with all your might
against a team on the other end of the rope, which is
doing the same thing. It's a struggle of strength and
will. Do you do that with God? Are you struggling
against Him to have your way in your life? If so, you
probably are not trusting Him.

Trusting God means that your will for your life is
becoming aligned with His. You aren't struggling to
have your way because you have submitted to Him.
Then God will give you the desires of your heart –
more than likely that will be the desire to know Him
better and to serve Him fully.

A Great Stabilizer

Let us fix our eyes on Jesus, the author and perfecter of our faith, who for the joy set before him endured the cross, scorning its shame, and sat down at the right hand of the throne of God.

Hebrews 12:2

A gymnast stands on a four-inch wide balance beam and spins around ... without falling off! Then she continues her routine of jumping, flipping and dancing on the beam. How does she spin and not get dizzy? How does she know when she has done two rotations? "Simple," she says, "I just fix my eyes on an object in front of me. It's my stabilizer. I count my rotations by how many times I pass it." Yeah, simple. But an interesting lesson on trusting.

Fix your eyes on Jesus. Lock your eyes on Him, then He will be the stabilizing factor no matter what else goes on in your life.

The Only Safe Place

The eternal God is your refuge,
and underneath are the everlasting arms.

Deuteronomy 33:27

God is the only safe place to put your trust. Do you sometimes have your doubts about that? That's all right, but just review what you know about Him. Remember how He took care of His people in Scripture – time after time – even when they didn't really obey Him or stay true to Him.

Now, review what He has done for you and your loved ones. Do you see a thread of His faithfulness running through your life? Can you recall times when you didn't know where He was, but as you look back, His care is obvious?

God is trustworthy. You can run to Him and hide in His love. You can trust Him to hold you up with those amazingly strong arms, regardless of what comes into your life. You can trust Him because He loves you.

Have Your Way, God

"I am the LORD's servant," Mary answered. "May it be to me as you have said." Then the angel left her.

Luke 1:38

Picture this ... Young Mary, probably a teenager, is suddenly informed that she's going to have a baby. She knows the gossip this will bring since she isn't married. She knows this situation is going to cause problems, possibly even with her fiancé and her family.

What incredible trust Mary showed when she responded to the angel, essentially saying, "Whatever God wants is fine with me. I trust Him with my future and with my life." Could you do that? Could you say, "Okay, God, do whatever You want." Could you say it (and mean it) even if you couldn't logically see any way the situation could work out for your good? Could you trust Him that much?

Taste and Trust

Taste and see that the LORD is good; blessed
is the man who takes refuge in him. Fear the LORD,
you his saints, for those who fear him lack nothing.

Psalm 34:8-9

We don't hear much these days about fearing God.
Instead, we talk about how God loves us and is our
friend. But it's dangerous to forget His awesome power,
His jealousy for our love and attention, and the coming
accountability for who or what reigns in our hearts.

What's awesome is that fearing God, giving Him
the respect He deserves, being in awe of Him, and
recognizing His power, results in God giving us
everything we need. (Notice that the verse does not
say He gives us everything we want.)

Once we have tasted what God has to offer, why
would we look anywhere else for fulfillment? Why
wouldn't we trust Him?

Trust and Praise

O Lord, you are my God; I will exalt
you and praise your name, for in
perfect faithfulness you have done
marvelous things, things planned long ago.

Isaiah 25:1

Trust is a strange thing. You can't just decide to trust someone, even God, and, boom – it happens. You must believe that the person you're trusting is worthy of your trust. In those "silent times" when you can't seem to connect with God, it may be harder to trust Him. What's the remedy? Look back. Look through Scripture and see God's faithfulness to His people. Look back at how God has always been there in your life, even when you couldn't see His hand.

God is faithful and will continue working out the plans He laid out long ago. The better you know Him the more you will be able to trust Him because you will know His heart.

Second Chances

Because of the LORD's great love we
are not consumed, for his compassions
never fail. They are new every
morning; great is your faithfulness.

Lamentations 3:22-23

So you messed up big time. You wake up filled with regret and guilt. You feel so bad that you don't even want to face God. How can you keep asking Him to forgive you for the same sins you have confessed over and over, determined never to commit again. But before you knew it, you did them again.

How? Simple answer ... He loves you. As far as He is concerned, every day is a second chance for you, because His compassion is new every day.

Wow! Since God loves you that much, you can certainly trust Him to stick with you, every single day.

Who Is in the Driver's Seat?

Then Jesus declared, "I am the bread of life.
He who comes to me will never go hungry,
and he who believes in me will never be thirsty."

John 6:35

Do you believe this verse? Really believe it? Do you trust Jesus enough to believe that coming to Him means you will never want for anything?

Jesus is promising to supply all your needs ... not your wants, but your needs. You will never again hunger for hope and love. You will never again thirst for meaning in your life.

Of course, the key to this is in the phrase *He who comes to me*. What does it mean to come to Jesus? It means letting go of your control of your life. It means putting Him in control, letting Him guide and direct you and trusting that He will do that in love.

The Safest Place

When I am afraid, I will trust in you. In God,
whose word I praise, in God I trust; I will not
be afraid. What can mortal man do to me?

Psalm 56:3-4

Have you ever been really afraid? Not the childish
fear of a boogeyman under your bed, but fear of what
the future holds or doesn't hold. Fear of what another
person may or may not do. Fear that someone you
trust is going to let you down.

Where do you turn when fear starts to grab your
heart and hold you captive?

The steadiest place in all of the universe is God.
He never changes. He loves you unconditionally. He
can be trusted. When you are afraid, trust God to
protect you and care for you. Nothing can happen
to you that He doesn't already know about.

Trusting Christ

The Spirit of the LORD will rest on him – the Spirit of wisdom and of understanding, the Spirit of counsel and of power, the Spirit of knowledge and of the fear of the LORD – and he will delight in the fear of the LORD.

Isaiah 11:2-3

This prophecy tells us a lot about Jesus, and understanding it inspires our trust in Him. Look at the characteristics described here. Jesus embodies all the wisdom and understanding of God. He has the Spirit of counsel and power. He has knowledge.

Think about that. He can counsel and direct our lives. We can trust Him because He is God. He can handle whatever life throws at us.

We know He loves us, and these verses affirm that His wisdom, power and knowledge can be trusted.

No Fear!

> If we are thrown into the blazing furnace,
> the God we serve is able to save us from it,
> and he will rescue us from your hand, O king.
> But even if he does not, we want you to know,
> O king, that we will not serve your gods or
> worship the image of gold you have set up.

Daniel 3:17-18

When the rubber meets the road, where does your trust in God end up? You may never have to put your life on the line for your faith, as the boys in Daniel 3 did, but you will have other choices.

Choosing honesty – telling the truth on your taxes; choosing purity in relationships; choosing to admit your faith, even if it might cost you the "respect" of your peers.

Do you trust God to get you through these things? Do you love Him enough to take a stand and take the consequences?

Quiet Love

The LORD your God is with you, he is
mighty to save. He will take great delight
in you; he will quiet you with his love,
he will rejoice over you with his singing.

Zephaniah 3:17

Do you sometimes feel alone especially when you're in the middle of the struggles of life?

You're not alone. God is with you, even if you are struggling so much that you can't sense His presence. How do you handle problems? Does your mind race back and forth looking for answers? Does your heart beat frantically and your breath come in short gasps?

God wants you to trust Him. He wants to settle you – quiet you. Rest in His love – and listen for the music of His delight.

No Worries

"Do not let your hearts be troubled.
Trust in God; trust also in me."

John 14:1

Jesus went on in this message to affirm that He is the way, the truth and the life. No one comes to the Father except through Him.

He knew that life was going to be troubling sometimes. He knew we would have problems and that some of them would even come because of our faith in Him. He didn't say that He would take the problems away. He did say we could trust Him to walk through them with us. He wanted us to know that whatever happens, our faith and trust in Him is worth it.

We have the hope of heaven in our future and the promise of His help right now. When we keep our eyes on Him, there is no reason for worry.

A Mighty Faith

"I tell you the truth, if you have faith as small as a mustard seed, you can say to this mountain, 'Move from here to there'; and it will move. Nothing will be impossible for you."

Matthew 17:20

Faith is the bottom line. If you believe who God is; what Christ did for you; if you believe God's power; if you believe the Bible – nothing is impossible for you. Faith is a powerful thing ... even a little bit of faith. Faith that is as tiny as a mustard seed – that's tinier than your littlest fingertip – can move a mountain.

Unless you've been rearranging the Rocky Mountains, you probably haven't even begun to tap the possibilities of faith in Christ.

Faith and trust go hand in hand. Believe who He is, let your faith and trust in Him grow, and see what He will do through you!

The Bottom Line

"Therefore I tell you, do not worry about your life, what you will eat or drink; or about your body, what you will wear. Is not life more important than food, and the body more important than clothes?"

Matthew 6:25

So much time and energy is spent worrying about the "stuff" of life. Seriously think about the time we expend on material things such as food, clothing, home and stuff to put inside our homes.

We all worry about these things, but they are not what's really important in life. Our relationship with and service to God is truly more important than these things.

The bottom line question is whether we trust God to take care of these material things. Are we willing to live by His standards and with what He supplies for us and give our energy and time to more important things?

Heart Placement

Do not love the world or anything in
the world. If anyone loves the world,
the love of the Father is not in him.

1 John 2:15

You can't straddle the fence. You can't keep one foot in the world and put one foot in God's Kingdom. You'll split in two. Loving the world means placing supreme value in what people think of you. It means placing importance on what status you reach in your career; how much money you earn; how big your home is; how much jewelry you own ... well, you get the idea.

Loving the world and loving God cannot coexist. Being filled with the love of the Father motivates you to serve Him and love others. Those two things become more important than anything else. You can't proclaim your trust in God if you haven't worked this issue out. Where's your heart?

God's Word

The unfolding of your words gives light;
it gives understanding to the simple.

Psalm 119:130

It is difficult to trust someone you don't really know. As our relationship with God grows we learn to trust Him more. How do we establish this relationship? It can only be established by knowing God. We learn to know Him by reading His Word.

God speaks to us through His Word, revealing His character, His love for us, and His direction for our lives.

So, it only makes sense that for our trust in God to grow deeper, we must spend time in His Word, finding His guidance and direction and understanding His love.

Let Go!

"For nothing is impossible with God."

Luke 1:37

Did you get that? Read that verse again ... and again. Nothing, absolutely nothing is impossible when God is involved. So, what's the issue with trusting Him? Do you question whether He loves you? His Word is filled, cover to cover, with His declarations of love. He shows you His love in a multitude of ways every single day.

Do you fear that some things may simply be too big for Him? Some challenges may be too hard for Him to handle? Read the verse again – *nothing* is impossible with God.

The issue of trusting Him is more that He might not do things the way you want them done, right? Well, He may not. But He sees a bigger picture than you do. So, let go and trust Him – remember, He can handle whatever comes up. Nothing is impossible with Him.

Sticking Together

I long to see you so that I may impart
to you some spiritual gift to make you
strong – that is, that you and I may be
mutually encouraged by each other's faith.

Romans 1:11-12

Life is not meant to be lived alone. God is pleased when we live in community – with friends and family. One reason for this is that we can encourage one another.

Trusting is not easy when the tough times seem to go on and on. Friends and family can encourage you to hang in there. When your own faith is stretched to the limit, a friend's faith can hold you up until you get back on your spiritual feet.

When two people trust together, walking side by side, their faith is twice as strong. Don't try to go it alone. Let others encourage you.

Short-Term Winners

Do not fret because of evil men or be
envious of those who do wrong; for like
the grass they will soon wither, like
green plants they will soon die away.

Psalm 37:1-2

Does it sometimes seem as if the bad guys are winning? When you look at the world and see wars, poverty, abused children, the rich getting richer while the poor get poorer, prejudice, oppression ... and on and on, do you wonder where God is?

This verse reminds us to keep trusting in God, because the bad guys will get their due one day and God will prevail! Put your trust in God, because what He has to offer – the hope of heaven – is the only thing that's going to stick around.

The "winners" on earth will be the losers in eternity, if they don't put their trust in God.

Not Alone

"But the Counselor, the Holy Spirit,
whom the Father will send in my
name, will teach you all things and will
remind you of everything I have said."

John 14:26

We're not alone. There's comfort in knowing that, isn't there? The process of understanding God and learning to trust Him is not something we have to tackle alone. He sent the Holy Spirit to teach us and remind us of everything Jesus said.

We are not alone in the struggles of life. The Holy Spirit indwells all believers and works to help us become more like Christ by teaching us about Him.

How does this help with trusting God? We have a personal advocate helping us understand the Father and who helps us pray when we can't find the words to say. The Spirit's presence is another evidence of God's incredible love and concern for us.

Powerful God

Ah, Sovereign LORD, you have made the
heavens and the earth by your great power and
outstretched arm. Nothing is too hard for you.

Jeremiah 32:17

What would it take for you to stop trying to control
your own life and just let God have it? What would
it take for you to trust Him?

God made everything there is, from a delicate
flower to a powerful volcano. He made the ant and the
humpback whale. God made seasons, thunderstorms,
sunsets … and you. He gave you a mind and heart.

He gave you free will and a conscience. He knows
all about you and how complicated your thoughts
are and what your decision-making process is like.
He knows it all … and He loves you.

Ever-Present Love

Test me, O Lᴏʀᴅ, and try me, examine my
heart and my mind; for your love is ever before
me, and I walk continually in your truth.

Psalm 26:2-3

God's love is always before you. You can trust God
to examine your heart and mind; to know the deep
dark secrets that you don't let any other person know
about because He won't walk away. You can trust Him
to know what you're really, truly like and not throw
up His hands in disgust and walk away.

He loves you. He looks deep into your heart and
sees if your desire is to walk in His truth, even if you
repeatedly stumble and fall. He will pick you up and
help you to try again because when He looks at you,
His eyes are continually filled with love.

Magnificent Love

"For God so loved the world that he gave his one and only Son, that whoever believes in him shall not perish but have eternal life."

John 3:16

How could you not trust someone who loves you this much? God wanted a relationship with you so badly that He made a way to bridge the gap of sin between you and Him.

He willingly allowed His only Son to come to earth, be persecuted, suffer and die ... for your sins. He didn't have any, so when He paid that ultimate price, it was for you and me. Then God raised Him back to life and brought Him back to heaven to live with Him.

He worked out this elaborate plan because He loves you and wants a relationship with you. When you stop and think about it ... well, God is definitely worthy of your trust, right?

Remember Christ

Therefore, since Christ suffered in his body,
arm yourselves also with the same attitude,
because he who has suffered in his body is
done with sin. As a result, he does not live
the rest of his earthly life for evil human
desires, but rather for the will of God.

1 Peter 4:1-2

The way you live shows what you really think of God.
You can use Christian words, pray, tithe, even teach
Sunday school, but how you treat your co-workers,
your honesty, integrity, and concern for others, how
you spend your spare time, what's important to you,
those are the things that show what you really think
of God.

You are to have a Christlike attitude and hold firm
to your faith in Him. He didn't live for the praise of
people, but desired to do the will of God. Follow
Christ's example – trust God to be your strength.

Stay Focused

Look to the LORD and his
strength; seek his face always.

Psalm 105:4

You won't be able to trust God fully if you don't stay focused on Him. Keep your eyes on the Lord. What does that mean? Don't let your mind and heart get sidetracked from what is truly important.

Life is filled with temptations to put your trust in other people or in things like money or recognition. These will only lead to disappointment and failure.

Keep your eyes firmly focused on Jesus, seeking His guidance and direction daily, seeking to become more and more like Him in your attitudes and behavior. The better you become at keeping your eyes on His face the more your trust in Him will grow.

Healthy Trust

Whoever trusts in his riches will fall,
but the righteous will thrive like a green leaf.

Proverbs 11:28

This verse says it all, doesn't it? Those who depend on their money to get them through life are doomed. If you think your wealth is what gives you worth and value, you are sadly mistaken. Your wealth can buy you out of some situations, but it can't buy your way into heaven.

If you respect others because of their status or their wealth, shame on you. A person with money is not necessarily a better person than someone who is less wealthy.

Your trust should be placed in God and in your walk with Him. He will help you make right choices. He will help you grow in love and concern for others. When your trust is correctly placed, you will thrive and grow like a healthy plant.

Unfailing Love

Many are the woes of the wicked,
but the LORD's unfailing love
surrounds the man who trusts in him.

Psalm 32:10

Unconditional love … love that never fails. Now that's something you can sink your trust into. Perhaps you've had experience with human love. It can be good, strong, compelling – but not perfect. Sometimes people we love disappoint us, sometimes they break our trust. But God's love is unfailing. When you trust Him, His love will surround you, and it never fails.

Trusting God means being honest with Him, telling Him about your concerns, your fears and your problems.

You don't have to fear telling Him anything because nothing you say will make Him withdraw His love. His love is unfailing. It is constant. Trust it.

A Good Fragrance

Thanks be to God, who always leads us in triumphal procession in Christ and through us spreads everywhere the fragrance of the knowledge of him. For we are to God the aroma of Christ among those who are being saved and those who are perishing.

2 Corinthians 2:14-15

What an incredible reason to place your day in, day out trust in God. By trusting Him to direct your paths and guide your thoughts, you have the opportunity to be used by Him.

Imagine being known as a person who leaves the fragrance of God everywhere she goes. Others will know that God has been in your midst by the fragrance you leave behind.

God will use you to be the aroma of Christ both to the saved and the unsaved. God will lead you in this process. All you have to do is be available to Him and trust Him to lead you.

Happy Trust

Surely this is our God; we trusted in him, and
he saved us. This is the LORD, we trusted
in him; let us rejoice and be glad in his salvation.

Isaiah 25:9

Trust is simple and yet it isn't. Your trust is going to
land somewhere. When a person recognizes her need
for salvation, because of her own sinfulness, and that
salvation can only come from God, then it only makes
sense to place her trust in God.

However, Satan is going to fight that decision
every moment of every day. So, trusting God is not
a one-time decision.

Every morning you decide anew to trust God
because He has saved you. You decide each day to
be glad in Him. Some days you may have to make
that decision many times, but it is a decision that
will always be worth it.

Your Strengths

It was he who gave some to be apostles,
some to be prophets, some to be evangelists,
and some to be pastors and teachers,
to prepare God's people for works of service,
so that the body of Christ may be built up.

Ephesians 4:11-12

Do you sometimes look around at other women and think, "What an amazing person she is?" Do you compare yourself to others and, in your own mind, come up short in the talent/ability department? You shouldn't. God has given you a purpose on this earth. He put you here for a reason.

Spend some time thinking about what you're good at. What do you get excited about doing? How can that interest relate to other people – building friendships or opportunities for encouragement? Begin working on your strengths and ask God to grow your abilities and to use you in works of service.

Formed By the Master

"Before I formed you in the womb I knew
you, before you were born I set you apart;
I appointed you as a prophet to the nations."

Jeremiah 1:5

God spoke these words to the prophet, Jeremiah, but they hold a powerful message for us, too. God knew each of us before we even began to grow in the womb. He set each of us aside for a specific life plan.

We're not here by accident. God doesn't waste energy with any action. He didn't create some people with specific gifts to do His work, but make the rest of us "extras" in the movie called life.

He loves each of us and gave each of us abilities and talents. We each have the imprint of His hand on our lives.

Wonderful Works

For you created my inmost being; you knit
me together in my mother's womb. I praise you
because I am fearfully and wonderfully made;
your works are wonderful, I know that full well.

Psalm 139:13-14

God created the whole universe by simply speaking
a word. He created the massive oceans, mountains,
and deserts. He formed the lovely butterfly and
the incredible sperm whale. He imagined flowers
of thousands of forms and colors, and gigantic red-
wood trees. He is incredibly creative and powerful.
And He made you.

A popular saying of years gone by is "God don't
make junk." Believe that. God doesn't waste anything. He made you and His works are wonderful.
If other people are tearing you down, ignore them.
Believe in your own self-worth. God does.

Not By Your Own Hand

For who makes you different from
anyone else? What do you have that you
did not receive? And if you did receive it,
why do you boast as though you did not?

1 Corinthians 4:7

You are different from anyone else on this earth. What do you consider your strengths – the things you're really good at? Are you proud of those things?

Do you sometimes look around at others and in your mind do a little comparison ... to see where you come out on top? Why? Nothing you have, nothing you are is of your own doing.

You have received every talent, every gift, every success – from God. So, you've nothing to boast about. You have only to thank Him for His work in your life and His gifts to you. No boasting. No pride. Just confidence. And thankfulness.

Inner Being

The LORD said to Samuel, "Do not consider
his appearance or his height, for I have
rejected him. The LORD does not look at the
things man looks at. Man looks at the outward
appearance, but the LORD looks at the heart."

1 Samuel 16:7

People form impressions based on others' appearance. We put a lot of stock in outward appearance. Those who are pretty, well-dressed, slender, "put together" tend to get our immediate respect and honor. But those who don't grab our attention, but may have so much more to offer from the inside, are pushed aside.

Well, God doesn't do that. He looks at the heart and sees what our motives are, how much we care about obeying God, whether we care about others.

So, that's the part of your being to work on. Be confident in the person you are on the inside – that's what really matters.

A Beautiful Spirit

Your beauty should not come from outward
adornment, such as braided hair and the
wearing of gold jewelry and fine clothes.
Instead, it should be that of your inner self,
the unfading beauty of a gentle and quiet spirit,
which is of great worth in God's sight.

1 Peter 3:3-4

Millions of dollars are spent by women each year
on beauty products and treatments, clothing and
jewelry. We want to look good. We care about our
outward appearance.

Now, there's nothing wrong with looking good
and taking care of your body. But be careful not to
put too much importance on that.

Your real beauty comes from inside – a kind and
gentle spirit and a heart that desires to serve and
honor God. Put your trust in God, rest in Him and
your peaceful, loving spirit will shine through.

Treasures!

For you are a people holy to the LORD your
God. The LORD your God has chosen you
out of all the peoples on the face of the earth
to be his people, his treasured possession.

Deuteronomy 7:6

Wow! What does this verse do for your self-image?
Even if you're in the slough of despair – thinking
the most negative thoughts about yourself – this
verse has to lift you up. You are among God's chosen
people! You're part of His family, separated out of all
the peoples on the earth.

The most amazing part of this verse is that you
are His treasured possession. You must have something
that you greatly treasure. You put it in a special place,
handle it carefully … take good care of it.

You are God's treasured possession. Ask God to
open your eyes to how special you are to Him and
how uniquely He made you.

Growing a Better World

Accept one another, then, just as Christ
accepted you, in order to bring praise to God.

Romans 15:7

Jesus accepts us in all our imperfections, selfishness
and all. He loves us. Knowing that He loves us, no
matter what, should give us confidence. It helps us
have a better attitude about life when we know we
matter to someone. It's incredibly special when that
someone is Jesus Christ.

That confidence gives us the ability and sensitivi-
ty to accept others in the same way. Acceptance
begets confidence which begets kindness which begets
acceptance. That will form better people, better
servants, and a better world where Christ's love can
be shared.

Recognize Christ's acceptance of you and make
sure to accept others.

A Great Plan

For we are God's workmanship, created in
Christ Jesus to do good works, which
God prepared in advance for us to do.

Ephesians 2:10

What is your favorite thing that God created? Sunsets in Hawaii? Magnificent snowcapped mountains? The massive beautiful oceans teeming with life? Delicate roses? Soft, cuddly puppies? Whatever your favorite thing in creation is, you do recognize that it was made by God's hand, right?

God's work of creation is amazing. He made incredibly complicated things and things that are simple in their beauty.

You are God's workmanship. He made you and not only did He make you, He also has a job for you to do. As He formed you, He planned what good works you could do for Him.

You're not here by accident. You're not in the job you have or the relationships you enjoy by accident. God has a plan. Look for it.

No Surprises

When I was woven together in the depths
of the earth, your eyes saw my unformed body.
All the days ordained for me were written
in your book before one of them came to be.

Psalm 139:15-16

Nothing surprises God. He knew all about you before you made your appearance on this earth ... in fact He planned your debut. He decided what color eyes you would have, how tall you would grow. He had a hand in the choices you made to become who you are.

While you toddled around the house at two years old, He looked into the future and saw the plans He had already laid out for you.

Nothing surprises Him, He knows the beginning from the end. So, don't forget to talk to Him about the big choices you have to make ... in fact, consult Him about every single choice.

He cares.

The Lighted Path

"I am the light of the world. Whoever
follows me will never walk in darkness,
but will have the light of life."

John 8:12

Do you sometimes feel like you're muddling through
in darkness? You're not sure if you're on the right
path, or even on any path? Well, there's one way to
clear up those questions – follow Jesus. He's the only
one who can illuminate the dark places in your heart.

By making a conscious effort to follow Him every
day, you will be able to have the confidence that your
steps are never in darkness.

Even if you can't see the path ahead of you, you
can trust that as you step out, the path will be lit,
because He gives the light of life. He promises that
you won't be in darkness ever again.

You simply have to follow Him.

Fearing God

Charm is deceptive, and beauty is fleeting;
but a woman who fears the LORD is to be praised.

Proverbs 31:30

This chapter of Proverbs often inspires guilt (and sometimes secret anger) in the hearts of women. This woman did it all! She was a good business woman, domestic goddess, and mother of the year all rolled into one. Of course, don't miss the little note in verse 15 that she did have servant girls.

Some writers say that the woman described in this chapter is actually the best of several women all rolled together into one description.

Whatever the case, the characteristic described in verse 30 is definitely the most important thing said about this woman. She feared the Lord. She gave Him the honor and respect that was due Him.

That's more praiseworthy than any of the other things said about her. Respect God and give Him the honor He deserves.

Finish Strong

I have fought the good fight, I have finished
the race, I have kept the faith. Now there is in
store for me the crown of righteousness,
which the Lord, the righteous judge, will award
to me on that day – and not only to me, but
also to all who have longed for his appearing.

2 Timothy 4:7-8

When you come to the end of life, wouldn't you love
to be able to say things like this about the way you
lived your life. You can, you know.

Paul made a choice to stay on the path – everything
that happened to him and every opportunity that
came along was viewed through the filter of how it
fit in with his walk with Christ.

He was true to his commitment to follow Christ
and, as far as we know, he never wavered from that
decision.

Good Use of Time

Teach us to number our days aright,
that we may gain a heart of wisdom.

Psalm 90:12

Your life should be lived so that you become more and more wise – with God's wisdom. Praying this prayer seeks God's direction in making good choices that will help you move forward in becoming the person God desires.

Each of us needs to seek God's wisdom in using our time wisely and being purposeful in reaching our full potential, in becoming Christlike and serving God with our whole being. That means that we will become more like Him so that those around us will see improvements in the way we treat others and in the choices we make.

When God teaches us wisdom, we can be confident that He is working in our lives and is pleased with our service.

The Best Choice

"What good will it be for a man if he gains
the whole world, yet forfeits his soul? Or what
can a man give in exchange for his soul?"

Matthew 16:26

There is nothing in this world that is more important
than our relationship with God. We spend so much
time on the "stuff" of life, the stuff that the world has
decided is important.

Even as children of God we fall victim to the
message that accumulating more and more money,
having a bigger house, nicer car, sky-rocketing career,
slimmer body, and all the other things the world says
is important are, in fact, important.

But those things amount to nothing in the face of
eternity. When you decide to focus your heart and
mind on knowing and serving God, you've made the
best choice.

A Focused Heart

These [trials] have come so that your faith –
of greater worth than gold, which perishes
even though refined by fire – may be proved
genuine and may result in praise, glory
and honor when Jesus Christ is revealed.

1 Peter 1:7

No one enjoys hard times. No one looks forward to painful experiences, but a greater good can come from the hurt and pain that life sometimes brings.

The realization that God is working in your heart and growing a stronger, deeper faith can put your difficulties in perspective.

When your heart is focused on worshiping and serving God in every aspect of your life, then even though you don't celebrate pain, you can rejoice that God is working in your life, changing you and making you more like Him.

The Worthy Life

I urge you to live a life worthy of the calling
you have received. Be completely humble and
gentle; be patient, bearing with one another in love.

Ephesians 4:1-2

Sometimes women seem to struggle with knowing what God wants them to do with their lives; what they should be doing to serve Him. They have trouble "finding themselves." Living for God ... and just living in general ... is a process that unfolds and develops through the years.

However, there is no real reason to say that you don't know what God wants you to do. There are basic things that He has made very clear and they are good beginning points in living the Christian life: the way you relate to other people.

The beginning of the worthy calling is to begin living in love with others.

All Cleaned Up

All have sinned and fall short of the glory of
God, and are justified freely by his grace through
the redemption that came by Christ Jesus.

Romans 3:23-24

So, you're not perfect – no one is. So you make
mistakes – everyone does. Don't let yourself fall into
the trap of looking around at others and thinking
they have their lives all together and since you
don't – you must be a failure. It just isn't so.

The Bible confirms that ALL of us are sinners. ALL
of us fall short of God's glory. The hope that covers
this depressing fact is that Jesus Christ paid the price
for our sins. His death and resurrection cleaned us up
and presents us to God as brand new. That's a fact.

So don't get down on yourself for repeated failures and sins. Look at the hope of Christ's gift to you.

Set Apart

Know that the LORD has set apart the godly for himself; the LORD will hear when I call to him.

Psalm 4:3

Do you sometimes feel alone in the world, even though you're surrounded by people? Perhaps you feel that no one seems to really understand you. Or perhaps those around you are caught up in their own situations or pain and they can't give you what you need.

The psalmist understood that feeling. He also understood that his choice to seek God, his choice to follow God, meant he was set apart for God and that God would hear when he cried out to Him.

Did you catch that – set apart for God. Set apart like a treasure, part of a special group. You are set apart for God because He loves you. He will hear when you call to Him.

The Best Love

We know and rely on the love God
has for us. God is love. Whoever lives
in love lives in God, and God in him.

1 John 4:16

It feels so good to know you are loved. When you
believe that someone truly loves you, that nothing
you thoughtlessly say or do can destroy that love,
you can rest in it.

The truth is, the only One who completely loves
you that way is God. He loves you unconditionally.
He sees the best in you and the worst in you and
loves you still.

You can trust His love. There's a freedom in that,
a freedom to explore and grow in your faith and
know that, even if you stumble and fall, He won't
walk away. He is love.

Thinking of Others

"My command is this: Love each other as
I have loved you. Greater love has no one
than this, that he lay down his life for his friends."

John 15:12-13

Getting your mind off your own problems can really help your attitude. Granted, it's not always easy to think about what's going on in someone else's life when you're stressed about your own – but doing so is one aspect of living out this verse.

Focusing on someone else, pushing your own wants and desires and problems aside to be sensitive to someone else is one way of laying down your life for a friend.

This is serving God and obeying His commands. A side benefit is that you'll feel better about yourself!

A Healthy Outlook

A cheerful heart is good medicine,
but a crushed spirit dries up the bones.

Proverbs 17:22

Have you ever known someone who seems to have a perpetual black cloud floating above them? Someone who generally sees a glass as half empty instead of half full? Such people aren't much fun to be around, are they?

When a person gets into a negative cycle, it's very hard to get out of. They begin to see the bad in every situation and can't find much to give them hope. Negativity breeds negativity.

Make the effort to find one thing to be happy or thankful about each day. In this way you will, day by day, climb the staircase that leads away from a crushed spirit. Rediscovering joy and thankfulness will renew your spirit and give you a healthier outlook on all of life.

Believe It!

"Are not two sparrows sold for a penny? Yet not one of them will fall to the ground apart from the will of your Father. And even the very hairs on your head are all numbered. So don't be afraid; you are worth more than many sparrows."

Matthew 10:29-31

When you cry out to God for help, but nothing happens, do you feel like you're on God's "B" list? Do you wonder if there are other people to whom He pays more attention – whose prayers are answered quickly and for whom decisions are clear? Do you feel that you get God's leftovers – whatever is left after dealing with the important people? Not so, my friend.

God knows how many hairs are on your head. He knows every bird that falls from the sky and you are worth far more to Him than they are. Believe it. He loves you.

Clean Up Your Life

Those controlled by the sinful
nature cannot please God.

Romans 8:8

Trying to please God without obeying Him is as useless as butting your head against a brick wall. The Scripture is clear that God is only pleased when we make every effort to live as a new person filled with His indwelling Spirit.

If you're feeling bad about your spiritual walk and questioning why you don't seem to be growing any closer to God, take a serious look at your life. Things may look good from the outside, but you know the attitudes and motivations of your heart.

If you're still living as the old, sinful you, filled with selfishness and greed, even though no one except you and God know it, you are not pleasing Him. Clean up your life, then stand before God and see what He will do for you!

Pretty Packages

"The good man brings good things out of the
good stored up in him, and the evil man
brings evil things out of the evil stored up in him."

Matthew 12:35

Don't you feel special when you receive a beautifully wrapped gift with ornate ribbons and bows? However, things are not always as lovely on the inside as the outer packaging might suggest. It doesn't matter how pretty the paper or how fancy the ribbon if there is garbage inside.

The same is true of a life. You can seemingly have your life together, know the right things to say and do, but if there is not goodness in your heart, it will eventually become apparent.

Don't waste time working on your packaging – spend time with God, confess your sin, seek to grow in Him, then the inner you will truly be beautiful and it will show through!

Relationship Busters

A quick-tempered man does foolish
things, and a crafty man is hated.

Proverbs 14:17

Quick tempers are like lightning bolts. They strike quickly, come from out of nowhere and often leave major damage behind them. A nasty temper flare-up can scar another person's self-esteem, damage a ministry, ruin relationships and leave you very lonely. Similarly, sly craftiness that attempts to manipulate others into doing what you want will cause others to mistrust you and dislike being in situations where they must work with you or even associate with you.

Both of these actions will damage relationships with others and service to God. Jesus said that loving God and loving others are the two greatest commandments. Keep your temper and your motivations under control in order to be the person God wants you to be.

Baby Steps

Therefore, we do not lose heart. Though
outwardly we are wasting away, yet
inwardly we are being renewed day by day.

2 Corinthians 4:16

How many times does a baby fall down on her way to becoming a toddler? A child first pulls herself to standing, then holds on to a table and scoots around it. Then with eagerness and anticipation, she steps away ... and falls. She gets up and starts the whole process over again – falling down over and over. But no child has ever given up and just decided to stay on the floor and voluntarily crawl through life.

We should have that same kind of perseverance in our Christian walk. Don't lose heart because of failures. Don't lose heart because of aging or illness or discouragement or anything else. Remember that God is teaching you and growing you into a likeness of Himself.

Love, No Matter What

Above all, love each other deeply,
because love covers over a multitude of sins.

1 Peter 4:8

Have you ever baked a cake, gently placing the layers on the plate to frost and just as you lay the top layer on, it splits right down the middle? Frustrating, eh? But you cover up the problem by piling extra frosting over that crack and smoothing it in – then there is no evidence of the problem underneath. Love can do that. We all make mistakes in relationships. We behave selfishly; we say unkind or thoughtless things; we just mess up sometimes. What can cover over those relationship sins? Not arrogance or pride. Not money or gifts.

The only thing that really covers the problem is love. Love doesn't intentionally hurt someone, so when the hurt accidentally happens, the knowledge that love is present will help the healing begin.

Patient Wisdom

A man's wisdom gives him patience;
it is to his glory to overlook an offense.

Proverbs 19:11

You don't have to point out every mistake that someone makes. Your patience in dealing with other people shows your wisdom.

Others will notice if you keep a score sheet of who did what to whom and how many times. After a while they'll find reasons not to be around you. It's better to be patient with others, as you would like them to be with you.

This verse suggests that patience isn't an easy thing. That's why it is to your glory when it is shown. Ask God to help you be more patient ... with someone in particular?

Ask Him to give you the strength to overlook things and to not even need to keep a score sheet. Then remember to thank Him for His patience with you!

Contentment

But godliness with contentment is great
gain. For we brought nothing into this
world, and we can take nothing out of it.

1 Timothy 6:6-7

Think of a picture of contentment – a baby who is freshly fed, burped, diapered and snuggled in Mother's arms. Contentment, peace, there is nothing more she needs at the moment.

Do you have contentment in your life? Or are you constantly striving to have more stuff.

Godliness with contentment could simply mean an awareness that each new day is a gift from God. It could mean understanding that all you have is from His hand. That can relieve the pressure to work so hard and allows you to rest in Him and be grateful for whatever material possessions you have.

Seek contentment from God as you move through your days.

Brave Courage

Be strong and courageous, and do the work.
Do not be afraid or discouraged,
for the LORD God, my God, is with you.

1 Chronicles 28:20

God is faithful. When He gives you a job to do, He will help you do it. He will not start you out, then half-way through the project back away and say, "You're on your own!" There is no reason to be afraid or discouraged because if God is on your side, how could anything or anyone possibly hurt you?

The hardest part of this process is believing that God is truly present with you. Review how God has met your needs in life, draw strength from those memories coupled with this promise – God is with you. He will not let you go.

Single Job

Fear God and keep his commandments,
for this is the whole duty of man.

Ecclesiastes 12:13

The busyness of life is sometimes overwhelming. You can feel as if you're just checking one commitment off your list before going on to the next.

Sometimes life is so busy that it's hard to find any meaning in life, even if the commitments keeping you busy are church or Christian commitments. That's when it's time to reassess your priorities.

The Bible says that the whole duty of man – the major work of man – is to fear (respect) God and keep His commandments. That means you must know His commandments and you must commit to living a life of obedience to Him. As you do so, you find meaning in your life by honoring and glorifying God in all you do.

Open-Book Life

We know that we have come to know him
if we obey his commands. The man who says,
"I know him," but does not do what he
commands is a liar, and the truth is not in him.

1 John 2:3-4

Don't gossip about others with one breath and proclaim that you are God's child with the next. If you choose to be disrespectful to others, don't try to witness to them later. Your actions speak louder than your words.

Proclaiming your faith in God but treating others badly shows that you haven't really given your heart to God. Obeying the basic commands given in Scripture is evidence that you take your relationship with Christ seriously enough to change your actions.

Don't bother with the proclamations if your actions don't back them up.

New Heart

"I will give you a new heart and put a new
spirit in you; I will remove from you your heart
of stone and give you a heart of flesh. I will
put my Spirit in you and move you to follow
my decrees and be careful to keep my laws."

Ezekiel 36:26-27

"You can't teach an old dog new tricks." Maybe you
feel that way about learning to obey God ... "It's too
hard to change old habits. I'll never learn to obey
God's commands." Well, the good news is that you
don't have to do this on your own.

God promises that when you become His child, He
will give you a new heart and the gift of His Spirit. The
Spirit will help you learn to follow God's commands.
You're not on your own!

Running Light

Therefore, since we are surrounded by
such a great cloud of witnesses, let us throw
off everything that hinders and the sin
that so easily entangles, and let us run with
perseverance the race marked out for us.

Hebrews 12:1

Have you noticed that runners wear the bare minimum of clothing? That makes it easier to run. If they ran wearing heavy winter coats and snow boots, they would quickly tire and not have a chance of winning the race.

The writer of Hebrews made a good analogy for us here. We're running the race of faith; a race that makes our faith deeper and our trust stronger as we run. So, we've got to get rid of the "junk" that can weigh us down.

There are no secret sins. You can't keep a couple of favorite sins in the closet and think no one will know. God knows.

Learning To Obey

Jesus replied, "If anyone loves me,
he will obey my teaching. My Father
will love him, and we will come to
him and make our home with him."

John 14:23

Love and obedience cannot be separated. Jesus said this over and over ... loving leads to obeying. Think about people you love – you probably try to please them and do things you know will make them happy. It brings you joy to do things for them. The way you can bring joy to God is by obeying Him. What's the best way to know how to obey Him?

You have to spend time in His Word, gaining understanding of what it means to obey Him. Resolve before God to open your heart to Him and allow Him to reveal areas in your life that you need to work on. Let Him teach you.

Deliberate Sins

If we deliberately keep on sinning after
we have received the knowledge of the truth,
no sacrifice for sins is left, but only a fearful
expectation of judgment and of raging fire
that will consume the enemies of God.

Hebrews 10:26-27

A fool knows the right thing to do but doesn't do it. When God's commandments become clear to you and you understand the difference between right and wrong, from God's perspective, you'd better obey what you know to be right.

If you continue to live the way you've always lived and try to justify your behavior with excuses, you're just fooling yourself.

Scripture is clear that deliberately continuing to sin when you know better, is a slap in the face to Christ's sacrificial death for your sins. You will face judgment for your deliberate disobedience. Don't sin ... obey.

School of Faith

Teach me your way, O LORD, and I
will walk in your truth; give me an
undivided heart, that I may fear your name.

Psalm 86:11

Your doctor probably has a diploma hanging on his wall signifying that he has completed the study program to qualify him to be a doctor. He has learned everything he needs to know to take care of you and your family.

The school of faith is nothing like that. You will only graduate from learning to walk with God when you get to heaven. As long as you're on this earth, your education continues.

Thankfully, God will help you in your study program. He even gives you a private tutor – the Holy Spirit. The psalmist prayed for a heart that would be able to singularly focus on knowing God. That's a prayer we all should pray.

Rules of the Road

I have hidden your word in my
heart that I might not sin against you.

Psalm 119:11

When a teenager is preparing to take her driver's license test, she studies the Rules of the Road booklet religiously. She doesn't want to take any chance of failing the test. Her focus, her goal, is to know that information.

We should approach knowing God's Word with even more eagerness. God's Word is our Rules of the Road for life. In it, God reveals His guidelines for the way we live among each other and how we relate to Him.

By knowing His Word so well that it is implanted in our hearts, we have a clear understanding of what actions are sinful. Know His Word ... it will help you learn obedience.

Get Rid of Sin

"If your right hand causes you to sin,
cut it off and throw it away. It is better
for you to lose one part of your body
than for your whole body to go into hell."

Matthew 5:30

Flip Wilson used to do a comic routine that always ended with the punch line, "The devil made me do it!" He used that little phrase to justify a myriad of bad behaviors.

Justification ... do you try to justify the reasons for your sin? Do you make excuses as to why what you're doing is okay?

Jesus said that there is no justification. He said if anything makes you sin – get rid of it. Sin ... disobeying God ... is serious. Don't knowingly let anything stand in the way of obeying God.

Long Term

The world and its desires pass away, but
the man who does the will of God lives forever.

1 John 2:17

We invest so much time and energy in the things
of this world. We work at careers that we mistaken-
ly think make us more important and successful.
We buy bigger homes that take more time to care
for. We desire more gadgets, more vacations, more
jewelry. We care so much about the world's standards
of success.

The reality is that all those things will pass away.
They will not last. The one thing that will last is our
obedience to God. We go into eternity with that one
thing. It is all that lasts.

Don't let the "stuff" of this world get in the way of
knowing and obeying God. It's what really matters.

Hold Fast

Be very careful to keep the commandment
and the law that Moses the servant of the
LORD gave you: to love the LORD your God,
to walk in all his ways, to obey his commands,
to hold fast to him and to serve him
with all your heart and all your soul.

Joshua 22:5

A cross-country runner leads the race. She rounds the last bend with legs aching and lungs throbbing. The finish line is in sight. She knows that she has a good lead on her nearest competitor. Then, for no apparent reason, she stops running. The other runners pass by her and finish the race. Why would a competitor quit when the finish line was in sight?

This warning from Joshua encourages us to keep learning about and obeying God. Give it everything – all your heart and soul. Hold on to Him until the day you go to heaven.

Surface Appearances

If we claim to have fellowship with him yet walk
in the darkness, we lie and do not live by the truth.

1 John 1:6

"You can't judge a book by its cover." That expression holds true for many things in life, and Christianity is one of those things. A person can know all the "spiritual" things to say. She can be active in church, teaching, doing women's ministry or singing in the choir. She can *do* all the right things ... but if she isn't obeying God in her heart, she is a liar.

How does this work? Obeying God begins in the heart. If she has private sins and attitudes that are disobedient to God, then all the "works" in the world will not make her holy.

Obeying begins in the heart. If you aren't obeying Him there, you'd better reevaluate where you stand in your faith.

Heart Occupant

Submit yourselves, then, to God. Resist
the devil, and he will flee from you. Come
near to God and he will come near to you.

James 4:7-8

Living in obedience to God is a daily battle. Satan
doesn't want you to win even a minor victory, so
you can never let your guard down. Submitting to
God and resisting Satan means not struggling against
the commands God has given.

Don't argue – that's what Satan wants you to
do. Don't try to justify your sins. That makes Satan
smile, too.

Stay close to God on a daily basis, read His Word,
pray, listen for His voice and He will come. He'll help
you obey. He'll help you resist the temptations and
tricks of Satan. Satan and God cannot occupy the
same heart, so when God is there, Satan has to go.

Classroom Lessons

"I will instruct you and teach you in the way you should go; I will counsel you and watch over you."

Psalm 32:8

God Himself is your teacher. God's classroom is the world and His subject book is the Bible. You are an intern and He is teaching you. Lessons are learned through practical life situations.

Your teacher is always with you to help you understand when you have learned a lesson and passed a test or not quite gotten the gist of a lesson and need to repeat a part of the course.

The guide book (the Bible) is always available to outline the lesson plans and give you practical help in learning the lessons. It's not easy to get an "A" in this class ... it takes some work. But what an incredible privilege to be God's student.

Everyday Grind

He whose walk is upright fears the LORD,
but he whose ways are devious despises Him.

Proverbs 14:2

Everything you do in living your daily, everyday life – everything – shows what your opinion of God is. Scary thought, isn't it? Think about the way you drive, your attitudes toward store clerks, responses to telemarketers, how you handle the children, your tone of voice when you speak to your husband, what you think about a coworker … everything you think, say, and do in a given day.

If you respect and honor God, you will obey Him and that will be evident in your daily life. A big part of obeying God is loving others – all the time. If your opinion of yourself is higher than your opinion of God, that will show, too. Fear God … respect Him and obey Him.

Daily Battle

Live by the Spirit, and you will not gratify
the desires of the sinful nature. For the sinful
nature desires what is contrary to the Spirit,
and the Spirit what is contrary to the
sinful nature. They are in conflict with each
other, so that you do not do what you want.

Galatians 5:16-17

Your heart is a battleground. The battle is whether
you will obey God or satisfy the desires of your
old sinful nature. Some days your old nature surges
forward and it causes you to live in selfishness and
self-gratification.

Other days your new nature is at the forefront and
you seek God's help and guidance throughout the day.

When those days happen, don't ever think that
the battle is won. Living in obedience to God is a
daily – no – minute-by-minute battle. Don't let your
guard down. Stay close to God.

Pressure Cooker Living

Though rulers sit together and slander me,
your servant will meditate on your decrees. Your
statutes are my delight; they are my counselors.

Psalm 119:23-24

How good are you under pressure? How about peer pressure? When family members, coworkers or friends tease you because of your faith, what's your response? Do you keep on living for God and obeying Him because deep down inside that's who you are and you can't do anything less? Do you compromise what you know to be right and let their attitudes pull you away from obeying God? Where do you turn for strength in those times?

The best place, as the psalmist found, was God's Word. Don't be influenced by those who would pull you away from God. Meditate on His words and find strength in them.

Tough Love

"You have heard that it was said,
'Love your neighbor and hate your
enemy.' But I tell you: Love your enemies
and pray for those who persecute you."

Matthew 5:43-44

No one said that obeying God would be easy. Jesus confirms that in these verses. Anyone can love their friends. Friends are … friends. You usually share similar values and morals. But enemies … well, that's a whole different story. Especially enemies who make your life miserable.

Jesus said that the real mark of a believer, a person who lives out God's values, is that she loves her enemies and even prays for them. Tough call. But not impossible because God never asks us to do something without promising His strength to help. Just ask Him and perhaps some of those enemies will become friends.

Basic Obedience

"If my people, who are called by my
name, will humble themselves and pray
and seek my face and turn from their
wicked ways, then will I hear from heaven and
will forgive their sin and will heal their land."

2 Chronicles 7:14

This sounds so basic ... but it's so important. Four
simple steps:

- Humble yourself (confess your sin and admit you
  need God's help).
- Pray (stay in communication with Him).
- Seek His face (take time to meditate and experience
  His presence).
- Turn from your sin (being in His presence must
  change you).

God promises to hear your prayers and to take
action on your behalf. If you ever feel at a loss as to
what obeying God means – start here.

Number One

"You shall have no other gods before me."

Exodus 20:3

Nothing should be more important to you than God. He won't stand for that. Is there something that is more important to you than God is? Think about it. You might not ever admit it out loud, but do you hold onto your children ... afraid of what God might require? Then they are before God in your heart.

What about your marriage, career, home, status in the community? What's important to you? Is there a secret compartment in your heart that only you and God know about, where you keep the something that is more precious to you than God Himself? This first of the Ten Commandments requires that nothing and no one be placed before God in your heart.

Are you obeying Number One?

Living Together

You shall not murder ... commit adultery ...
steal ... give false testimony against
your neighbor ... covet your neighbor's
house ... wife ... manservant ... or
anything that belongs to your neighbor.

Exodus 20:13-17

The second half of the Ten Commandments gives
clear guidelines for how to live with other people.
Treating other people with respect is the foundation
for obeying these commands.

Of course, you would never murder or commit
adultery, but what about the layers of behavior that
lead to those actions like destroying someone's repu-
tation by lying; cutting someone out of your life so
that they are dead to you; lusting after another man?

Some of these sins are often found in our lives.
Take an honest look at yourself. Do you need to clean
anything up in your life?

Be Like Jesus

Whoever claims to live in
him must walk as Jesus did.

1 John 2:6

Jesus didn't come to earth just to die for our sins, though that gift is wonderful beyond understanding. He also came to show us how to live with one another. If we study His life we will learn how to live as His people in this world. We learn how to handle crisis situations by looking at His temptation or how He responded to those who questioned His authority.

We learn about friendships by reading of how He interacted with His disciples and others. We learn about serving one another by reading of how He constantly gave of His time and energy to help other people.

We see how important Jesus felt it was for everyone to learn about God. When we study Jesus' life and try to live as He did, we will be living in obedience to God.

Active Love

The entire law is summed up in a single
command: "Love your neighbor as yourself."

Galatians 5:14

This verse cuts through all the garbage we sometimes produce in an effort to justify our actions and attitudes. Loving your neighbor is the clearest evidence that you are God's woman in this world.

Who is your neighbor? Remember the story of the Good Samaritan (Luke 15)? Your neighbor is anyone who has a need – even those who are "different" from you. That means becoming aware of and helping the undesirables, the unpopular, the enemy.

Loving these people doesn't just mean sending money to an organization to help them. It means getting your hands dirty, opening your heart, serving. Love them as much as you love yourself – meet their needs as quickly and thoroughly as you take care of your own.

Know the Playbook

Do not let this Book of the Law depart
from your mouth; meditate on it day and night,
so that you may be careful to do everything written
in it. Then you will be prosperous and successful.

Joshua 1:8

A professional football player would no more go out on the field without studying his playbook than he would without his helmet and pads. He would be lost when a play was called because he wouldn't know what his responsibilities were in that play.

The Bible is our playbook. In it, God has outlined everything we need to know to live a life of obedience to Him. If we don't study it, then we won't know what we're supposed to do.

Make time in your day ... every day ... to spend time in God's Word. The only way to obey it is to know what it says.

The Most Important

Above all else, guard your heart,
for it is the wellspring of life.

Proverbs 4:23

The writer of Proverbs has just spent 22 verses of this chapter on how to be wise and how to avoid pitfalls. When he comes to verse 23 he wants to make a point about how to avoid the bad choices of life. "Above all else" – more important than anything else I've just told you ... if you don't remember anything else I've said, remember this ... *guard your heart*. Be careful where you set your affections, watch what becomes important to you, mind your priorities.

Your heart determines the choices you make because it's very hard to go against what your heart is telling you. If you're serious about obeying God, put Him on the throne of your heart. Let Him determine your choices and the paths you follow.

Just Do It

Anyone, then, who knows the good he
ought to do and doesn't do it, sins.

James 4:17

There's no such thing as a spiritual gift of justification. Sin is sin. When you know something is wrong and you do it anyway ... sin. Plain and simple. You can give a hundred reasons as to why you did it or how other people can do it and it's okay, but if God has told you in your heart that this is not right for you, then don't do it.

It also works the other way – when you know things you should do, but you refuse to do them ... sin. Living a life of obedience to God means obeying all the information we have.

So, when you stumble, confess, repent and move on. Don't fight the process by justifying your actions. You'll never make any progress that way.

Learn and grow.

Drawing Card

You ought to live holy and godly
lives as you look forward to the day
of God and speed its coming.

2 Peter 3:11-12

Your goal in life should be to move toward becoming more and more godly. That means God's characteristics should be evident in your life ... to all people with whom you come into contact, not just your friends. Being godly is to be holy. Being holy is to stand out from the rest of the world by being moral, honest and loving.

You have a responsibility, as God's child and representative in this world, to know Him and live for Him so that people who aren't believers will be drawn to Him. Living a life of obedience to God's standards will set you apart from the world and they will see His love in you. That will draw them to Him.